POCKET BOOKS
A DIVISION OF SIMON & SCHUSTER, INC.
1230 AVENUE OF THE AMERICAS
NEW YORK, NY 10020

FIRST MTV BOOKS/POCKET BOOKS HARDCOVER EDITION NOVEMBER 2009

POCKET AND COLOPHON ARE REGISTERED TRADEMARKS OF SIMON & SCHUSTER, INC.

FOR INFORMATION ABOUT SPECIAL DISCOUNTS FOR BULK PURCHASES, PLEASE CONTACT SIMON & SCHUSTER SPECIAL SALES AT 1-866-506-1949 OR BUSINESS@SIMONANDSCHUSTER.COM

THE SIMON & SCHUSTER SPEAKERS BUREAU CAN BRING AUTHORS TO YOUR LIVE EVENT. FOR MORE INFORMATION OR TO BOOK AN EVENT CONTACT THE SIMON & SCHUSTER SPEAKERS BUREAU AT 1-866-248-3049 OR VISIT OUR WEBSITE AT WWW.SIMONSPEAKERS.COM.

LAYOUT BY WALEIN DESIGN
ART PHOTOGRAPHED BY MATTHEW MacDONALD AND WALTER EINENKEL
RYAN GEE PHOTOGRAPHY: PAGES 22-23, 46-47, 70-71, 184-185, 218-219, 248-249, 270-271
ADAM WALLACAVAGE PHOTOGRAPHY: PAGES 34-35, 102-103, 286-287
ADDITIONAL PHOTOGRAPHY: ROGER BAGLEY, REDMOWHAWK GEOFF, JOE DEVITO, MARK WEISS, CLAY PATRICK, JEFF TAYLOR, BAM & MISSY MARGERA

MANUFACTURED IN THE UNITED STATES OF AMERICA
FIRST EDITION
10  9  8  7  6  5  4  3  2

ISBN 978-1-4391-4773-3
ISBN 978-1-4391-6652-9 (EBOOK)

# SERIOUS AS DOG DIRT

**POCKET BOOKS**

MTV | BOOKS

**NEW YORK    LONDON    TORONTO    SYDNEY**

**Margera takes a break** from producing a video for his brother's ba

# Making the leap

m Margera, 21, of Chester County, has made a com

### By Robert Moran
INQUIRER STAFF WRITER

Let's go to the tape: Bam Margera, 21, is about to leap off a Wilmington-area bridge into a river 50 feet below. Taking a page from the Wile E. Coyote book of famous stunts, he is holding an open picnic umbrella.

Of course, he drops like a stone, screaming an expletive as he tilts forward into an unintended belly flop.

"I was hoping to float like Mary Poppins," Margera concedes ruefully, "but it didn't work out so well."

MTV's *Jackass*, the ar of stupid-human trick

But it more than p era, a high school dr enough from skati drive a black 1996 A Audi S4, and to coug payment recently f wooded enclave not hometown just outsi

His success is tes popularity and influ now a $900 million sport of the ESPN X

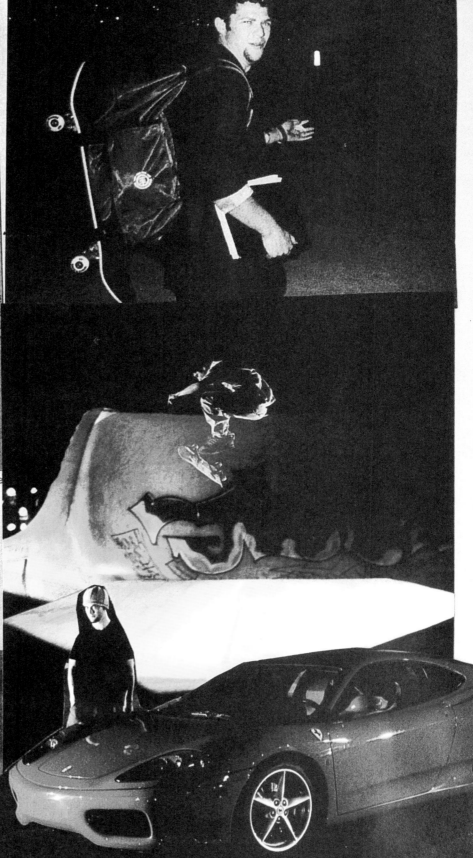

, to practice his skateboarding skills.

# to fame

e living off skateboarding.

oes cavalcade
ter wit.
lls for Marg-
no now earns
rsements to
d a blue 2000
100,000 down
house in a
his childhood
Chester.
the growing
kateboarding,
d the anchor
ich start next

**Margera** is a s

BAM AT STOCKWELL

JANUARY
1997
robertkisson
@udel.edu
SUNDAY
MONDAY
TUESDAY
WEDNESDAY
THURSDAY
FRIDAY
SATURDAY
DECEMBER
FEBRUARY
1 snowboarded camelback
New Year's Day
2 skated launch ramp wit Mike, DAY, MARI went to day's with kooz
3 went to Froggety School w/ Lanette and olivia
megans
4 WOKE UP early Bombed the hill with Digity, Mic, Bird, ty, sue, mandy irene
NEW MOON
MEN!
7 Stockwell Skatepark
8 RADLANDS (NORTH HAMPTON)
9 Fuck
10 Southbank and London (photos w/ wig)
11 London photos w/ wig
LONDON
LONDON
13 went to Bristol
14
15
16 Harrow
17
18
19
20 Liverpool
21
22
23
24
25
Birthday (Observed)
Glen E. Friedman
LONDON
photos w/ Daniel
26 Stockwell skatepark
27 skated LONDON photos w/ wig
28
29 Radlands
30
31
Bob Dole
Likes Men
This sentence has been placed here for no apparent reason
LONDON

# FEBRUARY 1997

| SUNDAY | MONDAY | TUESDAY | WEDNESDAY | THURSDAY | FRIDAY | SATURDAY |
|---|---|---|---|---|---|---|
| JANUARY | MARCH | | | Ryan Gee (215) ... Dan Wolfe ... wallasavage (@) ... robenckson ... mick vocovich 619 ... scotty wyna ... wig 0973 ... skip #1 ... sturt 619 ... kyle 617 ... | | **1** Shred For Life |
| **2** hung out w/chris Hanna, phil did 101 sit ups gee + manser mike joe, rasla, mark stopped homade pizza on produce. Groundhog Day | **3** Went to DOE → Make, cantake ryan doon ... | **4** went to east visited brandon watched wallrats w/ chris, mark and jess went to bolestone wrote film w/ chris OIL PLAYED, WATCHED WALLRATS | **5** Went to Mall w/brandon wrote more of the FILM w/chris H. | **6** went to reading w/ mark, chris + phil skated MAGIC brandon camcover wrote more of the movie / went to wc order | **7** went to glass co produce junction, dollar store, home, dry ice, picked up rash, went home Burger King UNDERCOVER PARTY w/oil went to dennys NEW MOON | **8** Filmed at ARTS |
| **9** went up chris/rash robenckson came over w/ joe. Filmed skatest brian at arts went home to chill back to arts | **10** mikes, burger king with geraw, bran and chris went to Joes around round | **11** Fairmans, Quarry, arts, movie place watched kids w/ brandl + chris **40** Mardi Gras | **12** got TM package skated at east w/ clark hanna jess dug treasure at drive in w/ chris Ash Wednesday Lincoln's Birthday | **13** | **14** St. Valentine's Day | **15** HEY YOU the reader FUCK YOU chilled w/ ART |
| **16** Filmed coach team and rash scenes w/Joe + mike went to arts w/ kooz | **17** Brandon stand up Washington's Birthday (Observed) President's Day | **18** mike + kerry left for cali brandon stayed over skated with him hung out at Fairman brandon Jess, deron Scattergories | **19** Skated w/ Jayson went over to house with bran ery WCD | **20** Skated w/ Geoff Skated w/ Brian Scrible | **21** OFF Reading w/ Shnitu skated w/ geoff picked up chris went to tash + days drove around w/ chris | **22** Quarry brandon hung out w/ chris + moore Washington's Birthday FULL MOON |
| **23** Fairmans, skated with her Fairmans ham ... Lonestar brandon + eggs deron = Jess recording | **24** Skated Joes CALIFORNIA | **25** Los Alamos GIANT MINI RAMP (filmed w/ SAIVA) CALIFORNIA | **26** Birdhouse House skated w/ summer CALIFORNIA | **27** Shot cover drop in w/ sturt CALIFORNIA | **28** skated HB CALIFORNIA | |

OUTHOUSES

# MARCH  1997

| SUNDAY | MONDAY | TUESDAY | WEDNESDAY | THURSDAY | FRIDAY | SATURDAY |
|---|---|---|---|---|---|---|
| **FEBRUARY**<br>1<br>2 3 4 5 6 7 8<br>9 10 11 12 13 14 15<br>16 17 18 19 20 21 22<br>23 24 25 26 27 28 | **APRIL**<br>1 2 3 4 5<br>6 7 8 9 10 11 12<br>13 14 15 16 17 18 19<br>20 21 22 23 24 25 26<br>27 28 29 30 | FUCK IT DREW | MAKE | CANTALOE CFI or AMY | SCOTT VEELYAT | **1** Skated LA w/ Barley<br><br>CALIFORNIA |
| **2** Skated LA w/ Denny and Bowl (filmed w/ ortiz) BIRDLAND<br>CALIFORNIA | **3** UCI w/ Kosick<br>CALIFORNIA | **4** hung out at Birdhouse house<br>CALIFORNIA | **5** hung out w/ GRECKO and ALI<br>CALIFORNIA | **6** night skate w/ Kerry<br>CALIFORNIA | **7** PATCHES PARTY (drunk muska)<br>CALIFORNIA | **8** Skips Ditch BIRDLAND<br>CALIFORNIA |
| **9** NEW MOON CRUISED AROUND HB<br>CALIFORNIA | **10** BOULALA ARRIVED<br>CALIFORNIA | **11** Went to birdhouse Skips Ditch w/ Boulala, cairns, alan, Pete<br>CALIFORNIA | **12** GIANT MINI Hung out w/ RUNE, ALI, and ALI BIRDLAND<br>CALIFORNIA | **13** BERLYL AND SHIT (Photos w/ kosick)<br>CALIFORNIA | **14** hung out w/ Boulala<br>CALIFORNIA | **15** Photos w/ kosick<br>CALIFORNIA |
| **16** mt baldy whole pipe, night vhts<br>CALIFORNIA | **17** CATALINA IS<br>CALIFORNIA St. Patrick's Day | **18** LEFT FOR SAN FRANCISCO (chris senn's) | **19** Skated SF (Adrenalin house)      Vernal Equinox | **20** Yuba City skatepark | **21** SACTO w/ BA | **22** The Avenues |
| **23** Skated SF grinded double kink (filmed w/ satva) Palm Sunday | **24** FULL MOON went to DELUXE, took photos w/ LUKE | **25** JIMS RAMP JAM | **26** SF hills w/ cairns, greg, jamie Boulala, comine moul | **27** Flew to LA, went to big brother (jaime throws interview) | **28** Volcom (talked to relay about NIKE) waxledges | **29** RIVERSIDE Photos w/ kosick |
| **30** huntington pap w/ Jamie dry edges grind double Easter Sunday | **31** skated ledges grind w/ muska + strids Easter Monday | | |      Good Friday | | |

OUTHOUSES     **CALIFORNIA**

215 S 03 jimmy pager

APRIL 1997 — ALI CAIRNS

Wallacavage 215- 59
Shrinker 35
Pager 010

| MONDAY | TUESDAY | WEDNESDAY | THURSDAY | FRIDAY | SATURDAY |
|---|---|---|---|---|---|
| Alex Moul / Jackman close / Abington OPEN / OX / M / 15 03 | **1** Turn yeto (got package) CALIFORNIA / April Fool's Day | **2** war legues GIANT RAMP w/ Valley | **3** Skated schools w/ valley, boulala ed, moul, lowery, ortiz / night skate w/ reynolds and bobier | **4** GIANT RAMP / Filmed w/ deryl grogin / w/ Andrew reynolds + mike | **5** Toy machine Demo / go karts w/ zero team and people |
| **7** NEW MOON / HUNG OUT WITH THE BIRD HOUSE HOUSE | **8** fairmans / Cleaned my Fucking room | **9** Mall w/ 3000 / Joe + Jeff / Saw LIARLIAR | **10** macked Photo's / went to Philly | **11** Battle 'O' the bands / alishas house | **12** Get Nike Package / went to Yuccas / demo / went to richs / stayed at richs + hannas |
| **14** went to fairmans / ARRIVED / and to shrinker Gared | **15** She / w/ wallacavage / Launched My Car, drop in, duct bowl / footage w/ Joe | **16** Skates sons / hung out w/ | **17** went to Jaysons | **18** fairmans / went to CFS and ate macdonalds / went to als w/ mike / Saw CHASING | **19** went to Jays / hung out w/ kandice / stayed over Jaysons |
| **21** West End skatepark | **22** FULL MOON / First Day of Passover | **23** hung out w/ kandice / West End Skatepark / stayed at | **24** West End skatepark / hung out w/ / OIL | **25** went to Philly / hung w/ kandice / Arbor Day | **26** North New Jersey (Skated a pool) Timmytown / TM |
| **28** thanks w/ brian / to / Hey Hill / Tim + mike | **29** TRENTON NJ | **30** Philadelphia w/ tim / ALS HOUSE / startweather / TM STAYED | | | |

| MARCH | | | | | | |
|---|---|---|---|---|---|---|
| | | | | | | 1 |
| 2 | 3 | 4 | 5 | 6 | 7 | 8 |
| 9 | 10 | 11 | 12 | 13 | 14 | 15 |
| 16 | 17 | 18 | 19 | 20 | 21 | 22 |
| 23 | 24 | 25 | 26 | 27 | 28 | 29 |
| 30 | 31 | | | | | |

| MAY | | | | | | |
|---|---|---|---|---|---|---|
| | | | | 1 | 2 | 3 |
| 4 | 5 | 6 | 7 | 8 | 9 | 10 |
| 11 | 12 | 13 | 14 | 15 | 16 | 17 |
| 18 | 19 | 20 | 21 | 22 | 23 | 24 |
| 25 | 26 | 27 | 28 | 29 | 30 | 31 |

ROBERTSON 302 90 / C / R

OUTHOUSES / attn Steve Mills / Scott McEachen
man drive beaverton 97005

13

# JUNE '97 1997

| SUNDAY | MONDAY | TUESDAY | WEDNESDAY | THURSDAY | FRIDAY | SATURDAY |
|---|---|---|---|---|---|---|
| **1** Bloomington INDIANA | **2** cincinatti | **3** cincinatti | **4** South Bend | **5** NEW MOON Lansing Michigan | **6** Brighton Michigan | **7** Pittsburgh |
| **8** West Virginia | **9** Baltimore — hung out w/ Joes mark and brian | **10** hung out w/ Kooz and Brandon met at Fairmans went to New England | **11** Laconia New Hampshire | **12** Massachusetts | **13** hung w/ Brian (prank calls) went to Fairmans Seth Brian Golfed w chris H. | **14** went to ocean city MD. Flag Day |
| **15** OCEAN CITY MD. Father's Day | **16** golfed w/ Kooz / steve M went to Philly Park new wall | **17** ran errands went to the driving range Seth went to Jess w/ Mike | **18** miniature golf w/chrith harms went amy got golf balls w/ chris | **19** went to Philly Park hung w/ logan prank calls golfed + skated at stroudY w mike seth, brian wrote Adams party golfed at penn oak | **20** FULL MOON chilled Mike + Fetry skated Philly Park went swimming at 3 went to Manlys party Edited Joe skinned stark w edm | **21** Phoenix Bridge hung w/ Kooz Jen Jones party some party w/ swimming out w/ sue and Irene starked Summer Solstice |
| **22** Waterloo Estate with Joe Philly Park Swimming at ryans | **23** I cant Remember | **24** Jumped on trampoline went to granite run w/ brian hung out w/ ryan Joe Picked up irene St. Jean Baptiste Fête Nationale des Québécois | **25** ran mile w/ brian + Jess! Stereo and chopin at Philly Park Ryans Pool party | **26** in and out w/ gee and Mike went to ryans hung out w/ Jess and Jeron Rainu / Jim | **27** | **28** philly Park mike tyson fig mad heads at cris |
| **29** chilled at my house w/gee, mike, Hussi Iaene, radio, ryan, sue Blah Blah Blah | **30** Great Adventure w/ irene ryan, sue, alex taylor, nicole | | | | | |

OUTHOUSES

| SUNDAY | MONDAY | TUESDAY | WEDNESDAY | THURSDAY | FRIDAY | SATURDAY |
|---|---|---|---|---|---|---|
| | | **1** Portland oregon | **2** Portland Burnside | **3** hung w/ radio then bran, then mike, alyssa, kerry | **4** NEW MOON 4th of July Party at Philly Park  hung out at kims Independence Day | **5** Skated Philly w/ Kerry, alyssa, seber, Leo, gee Party at Jen Jones Marshmallows at my house w/ gee leo and everyone |
| kerrytown alyssa seber to angies FORD | **7** Fairman's hung w/ bran a cool fight in town hung out w/ reene went to sarahs went skating at Starkweather | **8** went to steves w/ KOOZ | **9** leave for europe | **10** OXFORD ENGLAND w/ Alex Moul | **11** LONDON ENGLAND | **12** LONDON ENGLAND |
| NDON AND | **14** LONDON ENGLAND  harrow skatepk and oxford | **15** HOLLAND BELGIUM AND GERMANY | **16** PRAHA PRAGUE CZECH REP | **17** PRAGUE CZECH REP | **18** PRAGUE CZECH REP | **19** PRAGUE CZECH REP |
| FULL MOON AGUE CH REP PLACE 600 | **21** BERLIN GERMANY | **22** COPENHAGEN DENMARK | **23** COPENHAGEN DENMARK | **24** COPENHAGEN DENMARK  STOCKHOLM sweden | **25** STOCKHOLM sweden | **26** STOCKHOLM sweden |
| OCKHOLM sweden | **28** STOCKHOLM sweden | **29** STOCKHOLM SWEDEN | **30** STOCKHOLM TO ↓ HOME hung w/ KOOZ | **31** hung w/ Fix went to Jackies w/ bran Joss  Gosler Fair | **JUNE**  1 2 3 4 5 6 7  8 9 10 11 12 13 14  15 16 17 18 19 20 21  22 23 24 25 26 27 28  29 30 | **AUGUST**  1 2  3 4 5 6 7 8 9  10 11 12 13 14 15 16  17 18 19 20 21 22 23  24 25 26 27 28 29 30  31 |

*OUTHOUSES*

17

# AUGUST 199

Marvgle ... 3648 ext. 10    trige may 212
Equipment/ Merchandise →    2 3-6 →
MFM- 4152    Michelle Morrison 78 4 6 1

| SUNDAY | MONDAY | TUESDAY | WEDNESDAY | THURSDAY | FRIDAY | SATURDAY |
|---|---|---|---|---|---|---|
| JULY<br>1 2 3 4 5<br>6 7 8 9 10 11 12<br>13 14 15 16 17 18 19<br>20 21 22 23 24 25 26<br>27 28 29 30 31 | SEPTEMBER<br>1 2 3 4 5 6<br>7 8 9 10 11 12 13<br>14 15 16 17 18 19 20<br>21 22 23 24 25 26 27<br>28 29 30<br>fuck the fuck off! | Every name chris Raap ever had<br>1. Kraz<br>2. Cantaloe<br>3. KOOZ<br>4. Case<br>5. Rabe<br>6. Chris Red | 7. Fix<br>8. Coot<br>9. Con Air<br>10. Cossutter<br>11. chwissywissy | Kooz Pager<br>↓<br>9631702 | 1 chilled w/ ConAir<br>watched slingblade w/ Jackie<br>Als Cocktail Party w/ Irene | 2 hung w/ ...<br>... met ... went to ... ryan han... went to ... till 600 a... |
| 3 Lenape<br>went swimming at steves<br>NEW MOON<br>FIRST KISS<br>chilled w/ michelle ran w/ chris | 4 went to BK w/ Jess, bran<br>... chilled w/ Nate Ryan<br>chilled w/ Middle Now Mark | 5 Watched scream w/ ryan Quinn<br>went ... Alicia's house ... | 6 skated w/ kerry Mike<br>DEFINETLY KILL YOURSELF<br>went to steves<br>went to Joes | 7 TOM PAGER | 8 chris Raab is a fuckhead and Friday night is so cool TGIF | 9 hung out Blind/nuenue guys.<br>went to phil w/ michelle |
| 10 went to Philly hung out w/ stevie Lavar and spencer<br>Went to Davins got dialer from Zak chilled w/ art | 11 Kooz needs ICE CREAM<br>Jugged w/ Jess | 12 went to Granite run w/ michelle<br>chilled at sves w/ Dave Mike | 13 fucked w/ shit at radio shack brandon | 14 went to Sam's w/ michelle then ryan | 15 fucking Party or something | 16 Swam w/ raaa<br>drove F... to Phill... |
| 17 red Lobster w/ Jess ryan KOOZ | 18 I gave a fuck<br>FULL MOON<br>went to Wildwood | 19 WILD FUKIN WOOD<br>SAW Heath Becky and Pete | 20 MALL + EVENT HORIZON w/ MICHELLE<br>TO DERON'S HOUSE WE WENT | 21 Errands w/ raab+Dom<br>Got wireless mic watched movie w/ michelle Philly/raab | 22 chilled w/ kooz. ryan childers house | 23 ryan n... Shoe...<br>went to Shawns party M... |
| 24 Photoshoot with Michelle deron Mark Joe<br>31 chilled w/ Michelle then ryan | 25 went to Philly w/ Joe | 26 hung out w/ Michelle<br>OFF ROADED WITH GEE AND RAAB | 27 hey dick HEADS<br>I GOT A NEW BED Kerry n ARE BAKE<br>GOLFING w Kooz, brian, Joe | 28 skated w/ mike, Kooz chilled w/ deron Jess, Kooz.<br>GOT THUNDER BOX AND NIKE CATALOG | 29 went to Philly w/ Joe +Mike<br>Dude, you're gay | 30 went to Philly skated w/ TIM<br>michelles party toutino w/ Jesse Tim<br>Amores |

Bank Holiday (UK)

OUTHOUSES

Q: Why is Everyone getting a fucking PAGER?    Aov.com    1104 park

Hey Fuckers it's TGIF

| SUNDAY | MONDAY | TUESDAY | WEDNESDAY | THURSDAY | FRIDAY | SATURDAY |
|---|---|---|---|---|---|---|
| Chrissy Farin (Mike) 503- 3 | **1** NEW MOON went to Tincum Skspark then to Matts in Maryland then watched private Parts w/ bran. Labor Day | **2** Philly Park w/ mal gato y do haircut and McD's w/ Michelle | **3** tied up a bee w/ kooz, bran, mike and Joe hung out w/ brian, shawn, kaz at d.r Gee brought Photos | **4** went to Valley Fucking Forge to Find out that their isn't shit to Film there. DUNN CAME OVER TO CHILL | **5** went to Philly Park hung out w Michelle went to some party | **6** went to Jens w/ Joe TALKED ON THE PHONE Fuck Jess went to truman + HANNA's Freds FIRE |
| **7** chilled w/ Michelle RAGED PHILLY PARK! went to Rita's w/ michelle went to ARTS then to Joes | **8** went to EAST then Gairmans Wallocavage came over went to Valley Forge w/ Kerry, Mike Joe + Adam then to Joes | **9** trapped Kerry in the bathroom, Gairmans w/ Kerry + Mike chilled w/ ryan dunn went to Williams w/ shrinka Lady willie w/ chris H went to eat w/ Deron + Jess | **10** to EAST TO TOWN to HANNA's to HOME to BED TO SLEEP. | **11** Picked up Michelle from school chilled w/ ryan dunn went to Emersons Party | **12** Filmed in Philly w/ Joe, mike, bouch, bouch Member Philly Park cruise night and saw Money Talks w/ Michelle | **13** Judged a Contest at westend Chrissy wissy came over Langs Party w/ michelle |
| **14** raab sent himself over went to Fairmans and Joes w/ Michelle Saw vtrope1997 | **15** PHILLY PARK FILM SESSION! Saw "THE GAME" w/ Michelle TO JOES, TO HANNA's, TO BED | **16** FULL MOON Fucking Dentist Community Service The Mall to trade Shoes w/ Michelle to Michelle's went to Jaysons TOP 10 LIST FOR ED | **17** FILMED AT PHILLY PARK PICKED UP MICHELE FROM WORK w/ SETH TALKED TO MICHELE FOR SEVERAL HRS. ABOUT GOOD STUFF! ♥ RAA SAID "I LOVE YOU!" | **18** philly park EAST FUCKED MICHELLE ★ | **19** Something w/ Michelle raab doesn't look twek anymore football game and Joes | **20** Community Service visited michelle at work Saw Wishmaster w/ michelle, deron, Jess, michelle emily Sue/ Shildren Party w/ michelle ryan dave |
| **21** restaurant festival w/ michelle and Philly Park chilled w/ Con Air K-mart w/ michelle and sisters saw CLUTCH | **22** went to East Skated Philly w/ mike, Joe, Kerry hit a 007 BMW w/ skateboard Logged Footy at Joes w/ Kerry mike and bouchon Autumnal Equinox | **23** chilled w/ Kerry Picked up Michelle from school and FUCKED today ★ ruled! | **24** worked on video at Joes w/ mike + Kerry hung out w/ Michelle this symbol means FUCKED went to Jays | **25** ATLANTIC CITY trade show w/ Tim, Gee, Adam emersons party snuck out michelle | **26** Philly Park (540) hung w/ Michelle went to Joes w/ Mike. BAMROD an early nap. | **27** community service Philly Park (Blunton Wall) (bucky, Agah, dove, gee, barbee) Picked up Michelle |
| **28** san michael Philly Drop In A party at my house ★ | **29** BANANO MICHELLE DAY PRANK CALLS w/ BRANDON | **30** School to Communitys to Pick up Michelle to home to Eastside marios to Michelle to ★ to home Bran came over | Note to Self - my girlfriend is better than yours! | | grandparents heard some uh, giggling | |

August

|  |  |  |  |  |  | 1 | 2 |
|---|---|---|---|---|---|---|---|
| 3 | 4 | 5 | 6 | 7 | 8 | 9 |
| 10 | 11 | 12 | 13 | 14 | 15 | 16 |
| 17 | 18 | 19 | 20 | 21 | 22 | 23 |
| 24 | 25 | 26 | 27 | 28 | 29 | 30 |
| 31 |

October

|  |  |  |  | 1 | 2 | 3 | 4 |
|---|---|---|---|---|---|---|---|
| 5 | 6 | 7 | 8 | 9 | 10 | 11 |
| 12 | 13 | 14 | 15 | 16 | 17 | 18 |
| 19 | 20 | 21 | 22 | 23 | 24 | 25 |
| 26 | 27 | 28 | 29 | 30 | 31 |

OUTHOUSES

JAN 4 '18

**19**

# OCTOBER

★'s FUCKED MICHELLE
Geoff
G.

skated w/ Mike

| SUNDAY | MONDAY | TUESDAY | WEDNESDAY | THURSDAY | FRIDAY |
|---|---|---|---|---|---|
| **SEPTEMBER** / **NOVEMBER** | | VOLCOM / Remy S / Mark CAFFEY / Newport beach, CA | **1** NEW MOON ← | **2** w/ Michelle / Picked her up, to Sussex, to dinner at her house to LIAR LIAR! to stadium grille to childers to ★. WENT TO PHILLY / Rosh Hashana (5758) | **3** NE PHIL / HAUNTED HA / w/ MICHELLE |
| **5** Hang out w/ Michelle ★ / TENNESSEE (NASHVILLE) | **6** MEMPHIS TENNESSEE / Graceland / to Nashville | **7** CHATTANOOGA TENNESSEE | **8** CHATTANOOGA TENNESSEE | **9** GATLINBURG TENNESSEE | **10** WENT TO E / TO BRAN / its w/ Jess / Set up drums Side w/ Jes / w/ michelle / chilled w/ |
| **12** Philly Park w/ Kang + ★ Michelle / chilled w/ Raab and michelle / to Joes | **13** dived over Mike at Philly Park / Boofs Party w/ Michelle / Columbus Day (Observed) / Thanksgiving Day (Canada) to Joes | **14** Philly Park + West Philly / to Michelles to Joes | **15** WEST END Skatepark / snuck michella out ★ | **16** WENT TO EAST FULL MOON / went to Jaysons w/ Michelle | **17** went City / Philly Pa / WENT TO E / Homecomi game w/ Mi |
| **19** ★★ / And the Mail fourmens (New Board) / to starkweather w/ Seth and Brian / to thomas | **20** skated City Hall and Philly Park w/ Gee, Joe, Seth Menscer and kalis | **21** TO EAST, CHILLE w/ BRAVO / KING'O'FUCK IN PRUSSIA MALL / NOTE TO SELF: / ALYSSA ARRIVES WITH AT 8:00 / CHRIS H. | **22** Scott T. Huf Auntry. NY / Took Michelle to Work / Made Video at Joes | **23** Philly Pa / Ed arrived over michelles forto | **24** |
| **26** To Philly w/ Michelle FASHION SHOOT w/ ED, DEANNA, MICHELLE, QUIM GEE, WILLANZ in PHILLY ★ / Daylight Savings Time Ends (2:00 AM) / HUHS u KDOZ | **27** Philly Park and Night City Session | **28** To Lehigh w/ Kerry, Mike, Ed, deanna, Gee, Wall Jammy and Elyssa / Nollie lip by me | **29** 9:00 am WC skate MEETING w/ Brian + Mal / to East / Philly / Jamie and Adam Arrives | **30** Philly Park and City / watched Footage at Joes / ★★ stayed at michelles | **31** 6:00 am skate missle Philly w/ Ja / NEW / Stayed at M Halloween baby by |

OUTHOUSES — AMC MAR
AMC 556 3 5 .4

# NOVEMBER

CRUSTY DEMONS OF DIRT
(WEST CHESTER BRUNCH)
TEAM— Josh Ball, Malgorlaydo, Aspite, Seth
BAM, Kerry, Neil wade, Dave V, MFM

199

| SUNDAY | MONDAY | TUESDAY | WEDNESDAY | THURSDAY | FRIDAY | SATUR |
|---|---|---|---|---|---|---|

**OUTHOUSES**

WHERE THE FUCK IS SHIT?

FUCK SHIT

| SUNDAY | MONDAY | TUESDAY | WEDNESDAY | THURSDAY | FRIDAY | SATURDAY |
|---|---|---|---|---|---|---|
| | **1** VISITED MICHELLE AT EAST. TO EXTON MALL W/BRAND PICKED UP RAAB FROM CFS WENT TO MICHELLE'S TILL 10:00 WATCHED A MOVIE W/RAWDUNN + RAABS FILMED W/BRAND, ART, JESS + CHRIS H. | **2** TO EAST. PHILLY PARK SHOPPING W/MICHELLE AT EXTON WENT OVER ROADS | **3** TO EAST-TO FAIRMANS. PHILLY PARK BROKE BOTH TRUCKS TO GEES TO WATCH A VIDEO THAT WASN'T EVEN FUCKING REC-ORDED. | **4** TO EAST FAIRMANS SHOPPING SPREE HUNG OUT W/MICHELLE ★★ WENT TO PHILLY (A PORTRAIT W/GEE) AND KALIE. | **5** PhillyPark took Michelle to work chilled w/chris R. till 3:00am chilled w/jess chris + Deron till 5:00 | **6** Went to Philly Park internet w/kalisand and gee MIKE VALLELY'S SPOKEN WORDS At SUBZERO went over Michelles chris + kim came over |
| **7** ★★ went to Philly w/Michelle skated Philly Park. went to gees w/Tim dan + kenny went to south street the drive ★★ home was fun chilled cause I spranned my fart at FOR | **8** took Michelle to work Fairmans Picked up chris from school - went to his house as Jill cooked a meal dan, kenny, and unity came over - watched austin powers | **9** to EAST RAINBOW W/DERON ANETHEMA FAVER SUIT AT FAIRMANS Went to Ashas w/ Michelle went to chris's | **10** hungout w/kalisdio ★★★ went over Jens and bikes | **11** Left for HAWAII skated kona + wall parks | **12** Volcom demo (at Waikiki) albin petersen + kalie Black Flys Party | **13** North shore (sunset beach) |
| **14** FULL MOON North shore (Surf contest) | **15** North shore cruised around honolulu w/dust + train gang stayed at klints | **16** chilled in Honolulu skated a pool w/Alan kalie mum and Remy and friends | **17** took a boat to an island w/Dustin klint, Jen and Patty | **18** Flew to Maui w/Remy, Clint, dustin Jen, kalie | **19** Volcom demo at mall (ground ditch) mini ramp demo (skated) drove to a huge mountain w/crater | **20** Volcom demo at Maui Park |
| **21** came home from hawaii Went to mall w MICHELLE + chris him + me came over hung out w Michelle chilled + crash Winter Solstice | **22** TODAY KICKED ASS watched a movie w/ michelle (aspie came over) raab came over took Michelle out for 1 hour | **23** went to town for shopping w/jessard Michelle dan W. and Aspile came over and w/ to mikes saw TITANIC w/Michelle Dan, Aspile, raab + kim went to Jum W/see dan Aspile | **24** Went to rainbow for xmas christmas eve Listened to cure from the chilled w/Jess + Deron Dinner at Michelles Went to My house (xmas eve party) gee came over went to Al's party w/michelle and gee in spartacar First Day of Hanukkah | **25** opened things Went to Michelles than to Pere house gee drew us Christmas | **26** The worst day of my life, then after 5 go it started to get better CRMALL w/Michelle saw american wolf in Paris, parked at the Boxing Day Mall | **27** Fairmans hung out w Aspile + kim went to Joes went to Nells neighborh w/unit in scott deron unit and scott |
| **28** Went to the BEACH and Mamamons w/ Michelle, Jess, Lisa and Mom ★★ went to house where mom was house sitting it was a party | **29** NEW MOON To The Brinn house w/michelle went to granite run and ran into her mom and sisters listened to Oil record in basement, worked on calendar | **30** Went to kinkos w/Michelle for calendar Fairmans, Maldonados watched sleeping w/enemy w/michelle watched chasing amy w/mina, Raab, kim deron Jess chilled w Raab till 3:00 | **31** Went to Family's w/ Jess and Michelle Went to Philly w/Maldonado + Jess took photos w/walter R.davidson chilled w/Deron Jess went to Michelles for New Years saw midget sings out went to Boots | | NOVEMBER<br>1<br>2 3 4 5 6 7 8<br>9 10 11 12 13 14 15<br>16 17 18 19 20 21 22<br>23 24 25 26 27 28 29<br>30 | JANUARY<br>1 2 3<br>4 5 6 7 8 9 10<br>11 12 13 14 15 16 17<br>18 19 20 21 22 23 24<br>25 26 27 28 29 30 31 |

OUTHOUSES

With the unedjucating combination of me skipping
school every other day to go skateboarding with Mike
Maldonado and getting suspended for drawing picture of
Mr. Nutting eating out mark Hannas ass I probably made it
to class on average of 2 to 3 days a week. I was so

and getting suspended for drawing pictures of the class
eating out mark Hannas ass I probably made to school an
average of 2 to 3 days a week, I was so behind with
homework and tests I felt it wasnt even worth going
anymore!

BAM @ B³ GREGORY

# March 1998

February 1998
S M T W Th F S
1 2 3 4 5 6 7
8 9 10 11 12 13 14
15 16 17 18 19 20 21
22 23 24 25 26 27 28

April 1998
S M T W Th F S
1 2 3 4
5 6 7 8 9 10 11
12 13 14 15 16 17 18
19 20 21 22 23 24 25
26 27 28 29 30

March 1998
S M T W Th F S
1 2 3 4 5 6 7
8 9 10 11 12 13 14
15 16 17 18 19 20 21
22 23 24 25 26 27 28
29 30 31

More skates: 717- -0-5 & Christie Fax (503) 6 1 6
BIRD- 9 0 7
SEBER: 717- 6 4-
(714) 7 0 5 VOLCOM FAX
LANCASTER SKATE PARK - 717- 8 45 STEVE MOORE: 6 -89
Tim (guy from tv show)
(714) 3 5 5 K a filmer in Pa
906 from vista
**Sunday | Monday | Tuesday | Wednesday | Thursday | Friday | Saturday**

I LOVE YOU! I LOVE YOU!

# April 1998

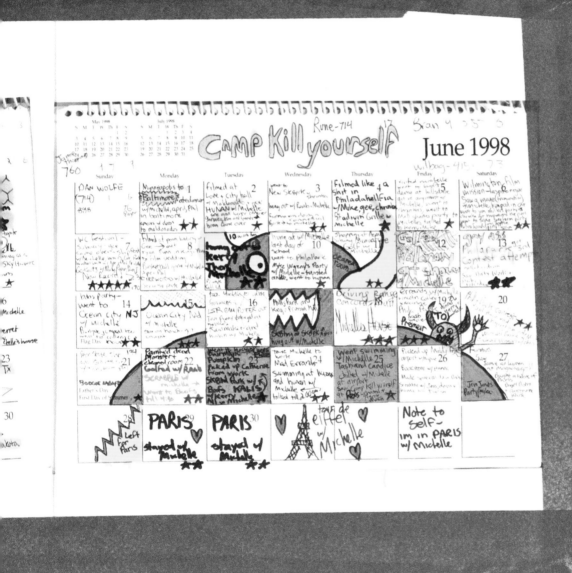

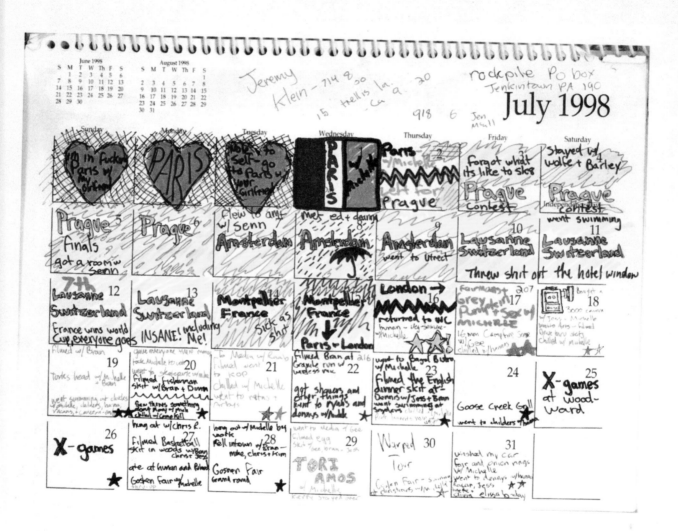

# July 1998

Jeremy Klein — 714 8...
rockpile PO box
Jenkintown PA 190

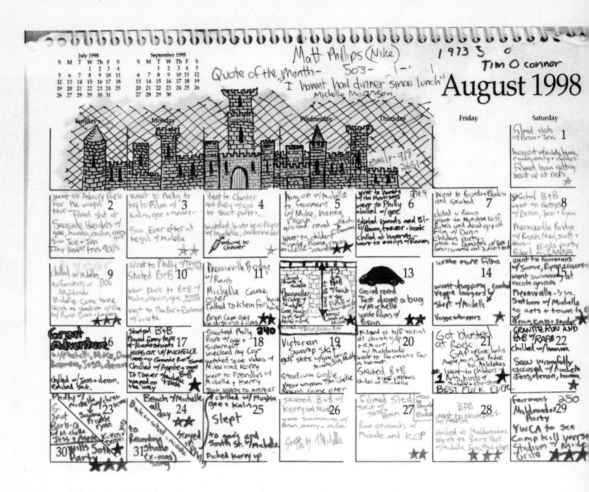

August 1998

September 1998

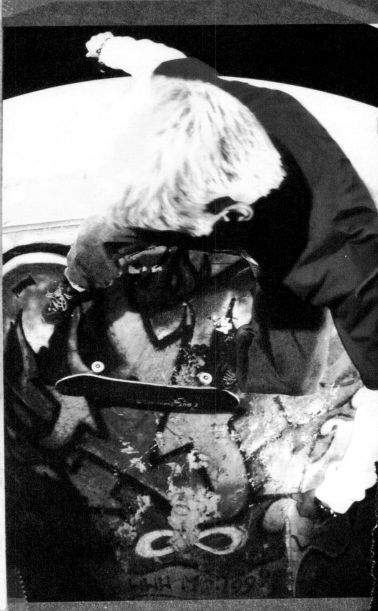

BK virginia fall

Punches, slaps + falls

Switch

1. Maldonado down the stairs
2. Maldonado hit w/ pillow
3. Jess getting slaped
4. Bran punching me about people
5. Bum punching bran
6. Bum punching bran + gee
7. slap + slap
8. punch
9. you got a bowling ball
10. dropping tv
11. Punching window
12. on the roof
13. I cant open it
14. Texaco slap
15. Texaco punch
16. Don getting beat up
17. Bran + dunn fighting at New years

Robahouse

24. Fan fall
25. Fan fall 2
26. golf fall
27. Media
28. punching bran at oakbo
29. englsh skit punches
30. jump into bush
31. umbrella jump
32. Bran Getting beat up

33. syracuse bed smack
34. Toys R us bran
35. Toys #2
36. Bran jump fall
37. Bran lawyer out

| September 1998 | | | | | | | | November 1998 | | | | | | |
|---|---|---|---|---|---|---|---|---|---|---|---|---|---|---|
| S | M | T | W | Th | F | S | | S | M | T | W | Th | F | S |
| | | 1 | 2 | 3 | 4 | 5 | | 1 | 2 | 3 | 4 | 5 | 6 | 7 |
| 6 | 7 | 8 | 9 | 10 | 11 | 12 | | 8 | 9 | 10 | 11 | 12 | 13 | 14 |
| 13 | 14 | 15 | 16 | 17 | 18 | 19 | | 15 | 16 | 17 | 18 | 19 | 20 | 21 |
| 20 | 21 | 22 | 23 | 24 | 25 | 26 | | 22 | 23 | 24 | 25 | 26 | 27 | 28 |
| 27 | 28 | 29 | 30 | | | | | 29 | 30 | | | | | |

# October 1998

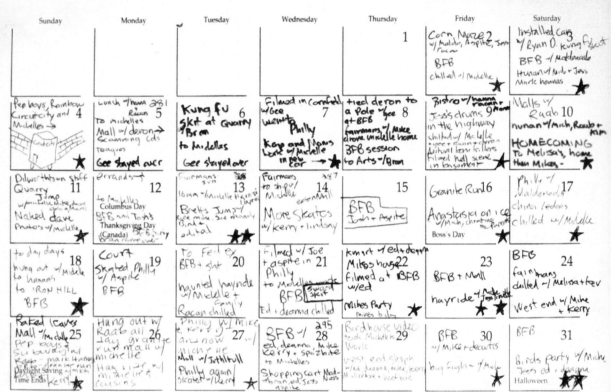

| Sunday | Monday | Tuesday | Wednesday | Thursday | Friday | Saturday |
|---|---|---|---|---|---|---|
| | | | | **1** | **Corn Maze 2** w/ Maldo, Aspite, Jess, Racan — BFB w/ Michelle — chilled w/ Michelle | **Installed Cats 3** w/ Ryan D. Kung Fu Skit — BFB w/ Maldonado — Hung out w/ Nick + Jess Mark hannas ★ |
| **Pep boys, Rainbow 4** Circuit City and Michelle's | **Lunch w/ Mama 5** Racan — To Michelle's Mall w/ devon → Scanning Cds To aqua's — Gee stayed over | **Kung Fu 6** Skit at Quarry w/ Bren — to Michelle's Gee stayed over | **Filmed in cornfield 7** w/Gee — Went to Philly Kap and Nons Lunch w/ Michelle in new car → | **tied devon to 8** a Pole — Gee at BFB — Fairmans — Mike drove Michelle home — BFB session to Arts w/ Bren | **Bistro w/ hanna 9** Racan — Jess's drums in the highway chilled w/ Michelle — spent racan + devon filmed hall scene in basement | **Malls w/ 10** Raab — nunan w/ Mich, Raab + Kim — HOMECOMING To Melisa's, home then Mikes ★ |
| **Dilworthtown stuff 11** Quarry Jump w/ paul, kellie, chris, devon, gee + hanna — Naked dave Photos w/ Michelle | **errands 12** to Michelle's Columbus Day BFB and Tom's Thanksgiving Day (Canada) BFB Gee Gran came over | **Fairmans 13** sun — 16mm w/ Michelle Higins — Bretts Jump w/ Gee, mike, Sea mandy Bird + ashtai ★★ | **Fairmans 14** to shop w/ Michelle ed on Mall — More Skates w/ Kerry + lindsay | **15** | **Granite Run 16** Anastasia on ice w/ Mich, christina Boss's Day | **Philly w/ 17** Maldonado China Ledons chilled w/ Michelle ★ |
| **to day days 18** hung out w/ Michelle to hannas to IRON HILL BFB ★ | **Court 19** Skated Philly w/ Aspite — BFB | **To Fed ex 20** BFB + skit — haunted hayride w/ Michelle + Comly Racan chilled | **Filmed w/ Joe 21** + aspite in Philly to Michelle's BFB Sword Skit — Ed + deanna chilled | **kmart w/ ed + deanna 22** Mikes house — Filmed at BFB w/ ed — Mikes Party mikes b-day ★ | **23** BFB + Mall hayride w/ Michelle | **BFB 24** fairmans chilled w/ Melisa + Kev — West end w/ Mike + Kerry |
| **Raked leaves 25** Mall w/ Michelle Pep boys + Subway w/ Raab — mark hannas Daylight Saving w/ Mich Time Ends Kerry ★ | **Hung out w/ 26** Raab all day granite run Mall w/ Michelle Hag ride w/ Michelle + cousins | **Philly w/ Mike 27** + Kerry and now Mall w/ Jethltrull Philly again skated w/ Kerry ★ | **BFB w/ 28** ed, deanna, Mike Kerry + spazbite to Michelle's Shopping cart Mall w/ hanna, ed, Jess aspite | **Birdhouse video 29** took Michelle to work — west end skips w/ ed, deanna, mike, kerry Michelle + west end | **BFB 30** w/ Mike + dewitts big Sugh w/ Michelle | **BFB 31** Birds party w/ Michelle, Jess, ed + deanna Halloween ★★ |

TY evans
619

**October 1998**
| S | M | T | W | Th | F | S |
|---|---|---|---|---|---|---|
| | | | | 1 | 2 | 3 |
| 4 | 5 | 6 | 7 | 8 | 9 | 10 |
| 11 | 12 | 13 | 14 | 15 | 16 | 17 |
| 18 | 19 | 20 | 21 | 22 | 23 | 24 |
| 25 | 26 | 27 | 28 | 29 | 30 | 31 |

**December 1998**
| S | M | T | W | Th | F | S |
|---|---|---|---|---|---|---|
| | | 1 | 2 | 3 | 4 | 5 |
| 6 | 7 | 8 | 9 | 10 | 11 | 12 |
| 13 | 14 | 15 | 16 | 17 | 18 | 19 |
| 20 | 21 | 22 | 23 | 24 | 25 | 26 |
| 27 | 28 | 29 | 30 | 31 | | |

| Sunday | Monday | Tuesday | Wednesday | Thursday | Friday | Saturday |
|---|---|---|---|---|---|---|
| **1** chilled w/ Rach Pizza w/ Miche, neil, hanna, racan chilled at home ★★ | **2** Filmed 16mm of shopping carts w/ bran, gee, Jess chilled w/ michelle and went to day days To arts for Voices | **3** Granite run w/ michelle developed film went to bfb w/ Miche Election Day ★ | **4** Granite run helped out w/ Art shit Skated w/ kealis, stevie Gee at temple rainbow records | **5** Concord mall Locked keys in car broke window open fucking brick Ged shit at Michelles chilled w/ Deron | **6** Skits+ 16mm w/ bran + gee Eds Art show w/ Michelle + Mayon | **7** chilled w/ michele Washington D.C |
| **8** Memphis, TN | **9** Little Rock, AK | **10** Arizona | **11** CALIFORNIA Veterans Day chilled at elissas Remembrance Day (Canada) Zoukala | **12** Skated HB w/ Reynolds, Kerry Sumner | **13** Ventura Contest jumped off roof | **14** Ventura Contest Toy Flip dinner in hollywood |
| **15** La school w/ Geoff, kerry, ed koslick, arto, deamn, muska Finished stills graphic | **16** Skated w/ Geoff, arto, ed, kerry, miker, elissa watched waterboy Hollywood | **17** to dave sheridans w/ erickson discussed Movie shit - went to dinner sandiego | **18** chilled w/ Jamie Skated w/ Ty, Mumford, Jamie | **19** Tum Yeto got boards Filmed w/ Jamie + Ty Smashed face in? | **20** Came the Arts house Went to Arts | **21** Fairmans hung out w/ Ryan Dunn Saw Michelle! Arts house ★★ |
| **22** bagel bistro w/ chris + team chilled w/ Michelle Ryan Oldies Arts ★★ | **23** Saw enemy of the state | **24** Philly Parts w/ Gee to shoot photos + 16mm chinese Food w/ Michelle chilled w/ deron deep impact ★ | **25** B+B did ged stuff at Michelles Stadium Grille w/ Michelle | **26** Michelle grand-mom to eat went to boofs w/ Michelle Thanksgiving ★★ | **27** Granite run mall w/ michelle, kathy, christina B+B Exton Mall w/ michelle + chris tine Prank Calls w/ Bran, Joe, deron, Jim, Sean, + hayal | **28** 3:10 SAW JOE BLACK w/ Michelle ★ |
| **29** Rock convention w/ Miche, Jess, Mayon Delaware caven w/ Michelle + Jess ★★ | **30** Punched brad in the face at K.O.P. Saw Alyson Nolan to Michelle's then Arts Joes b-day | | | | | |

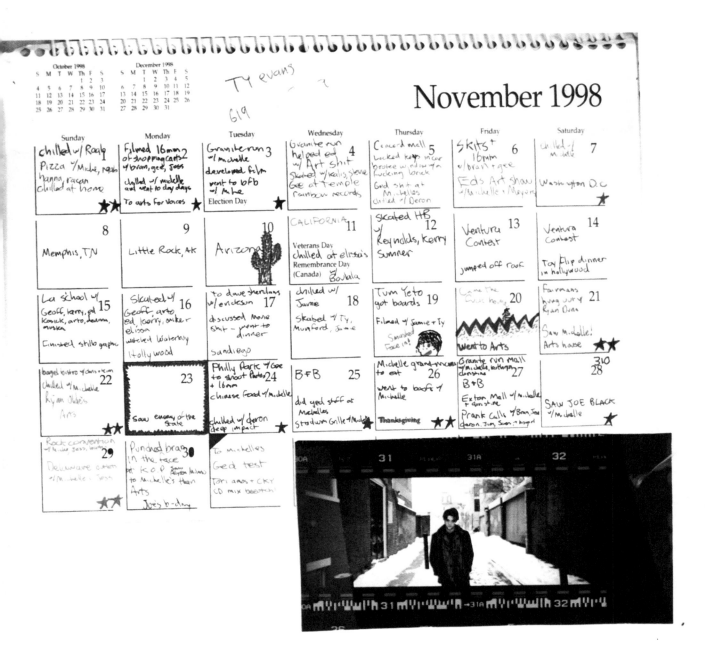

December 1998

BAM ~ 1998-99'
© RYAN GEE PHOTO

PHILADELPHIA

# 1999'

## HOCKEY TEMPER GET'Z

DONUT QUEEN

M, Inc. • Dallas, Texas 75238-1337

40cm x 50cm

| | | |
|---|---|---|
| breakfast w/ missy, seth, fanna  **3**<br><br>FDR<br>Practice for gravity Games | **4**<br><br>FDR<br>/ Leave for Finland<br>Independence Day (US) | **5**<br><br>FINLAND<br><br>Punched jean in the face |
| **10**<br><br>Gravity Games @ Fdr<br>NO DRINKING! | **11**<br><br>Gravity Games<br><br>film VLB pickups | **12**<br><br>Gravity Games<br>Pissed on Tom Boy<br>Party @ house |
| **17**<br><br>Ocean City MD<br><br>Autographs | drove home from **18**<br>Ocean City MD<br><br>WWF in Philly w/ Hulk hogan | EDIT HIM **19**<br><br>Ride bike to delu<br><br>Gables w/ missy + Jac<br>went to Jacks House |

**6**

Drinking Binge

Crawdaddys
Maximillions
McKenzies

**7**

RADIO BAM
HOOTERS w/ SHEIK

**8**

Rode quads
Borders (soccer)
chadsford tavern
Giant
more quad riding
sent tapes to MT

Al's Diamond cab
w/ Glomb, billy, now

International Women's D

**13**

**14**

**1**

BARCE

SKATE! SKATE! SKATE

**20** RADIO BAM

West Chester for One Day!

Antonios w/VLB
Hooters
Firewaters

Palm Sunday
Vernal Equinox
7:33 A.M. E.S.T.

**21** Flew to LA

RIGHT GUARD

Commercial
w/ T-OWENS

METAL SHOP w/ ville, gas,
Lyde, Alina

**2**

RIGHT GUARD

Commercial
w/ T-OWENS

Dinner w/ T Hardy
ville, glo

**27** Drank all Day w/ ville +
Jonna in LA

Red Rock,
Barneys beanery
Booze in
Hotel room

Easter

**28** Seth Builds Mansion replica

H·I·M

MANSION IN LA

RADIO BAM w/ FRANTZ
IN BURBANK, CA

Easter Monday (CAN)

**2** EDITED VLB ALL MORNIN

LA

Back to HIM
TO restaura

*Bus Stop*, Arizona, 1956

# ELEMENT TRIP 2000

Around April 2000 I met Joe Frantz at a Silly Bikini Bandits Film shoot. I remembered adam Wallacauge telling me about a guy named Joe Frantz owned a 35mm Movie camera and I was so impressed with that. I couldnt believe a random buddy owned an official m... camera. So I want up to Frantz during a lunch brea... and introduced myself. I told him I had $5000 in my bank account and i wanted to spend every penny o... a music video for CKY. He was into it and 2... later he came to West chester and we filmed... very first music video "96 quite bitter be...

# AUSTRALIA
## SYDNEY
## MELBOURNE
## BRISBANE

Ryan Dunn and I fly to Zurich with Glomb and
oger and we are here because, I am going to
ent a Ferrari for 4 days for $3,000 a day, o
mission is to get to Romania in 4 days for Red
wine out of Draculas castle in a small town cal
Brasov. Driving the Ferrari through the swiss alp
with one of your best friends was absolutely we
every penny of the $12,000 that MTU was stressing a
doing. It rained half of the time which pissed me
off greatly. It was such a boner killer like we
go to europe to rent a convertible ferrari
modena and if rains the whole fucking ti
So Dunn and I made the best of it and put
the fucking top down in the pouring rain an
decided to fly a kite like Benjamin Frank
The fact we put the topdown in a rainstorm m
it way more entertaining than a beautiful
sunny day. It was the farthest yet most sec
drive i have ever been on, we had only 2 cd's
listen to the entire drive which Dunn and I will b
every lyric memorized till we are Ded. Dead!
The bands were "the Beatzsteaks" and the new cradle
of filth, Nympetamine.

Once we got to Romainia I was a litt[le]
dissapointed just because it was a run[down]
3rd world shithole with powerplants a[nd]
rabid dogs everywhere, im sure half of [them]
have never seen a paved road. frantz was
reading some facts about Romainia and he [said]
the average wage of romanians per month is $7[0]
that is absurd! Bucharest pretty much sucked a[nd]
withe everyother town exept Brasou! Brasou i[s]
the tourist town that they dumped all there [their]
cash into, its such a cool looking gothic village, it
made it all worth it. Once we got to Draculas cas[tle]
we went on a hiking mission to the top to
get some Red wine, special red wine for the
Dinner in Venice. Dunn sneakes in as I wait
at the top of the hill, he comes back 5 min[utes]
later with 2 bottles of red wine, we are all exit[ed]
and ready to celebrate for our accomplésted missio[n]
I ask dunn "was it a pain in the ass getting the wine?"
he said "No, I got it at the gift shoppe for $6.99"
we hopped in the bullshitassshit ferrari and [took]
off to Venice!

B

SOV, ROMANIA

**0711**

ART WRAPPERS
@ MACH SPEED

Have A Bam! Day.
**Bam Margera**

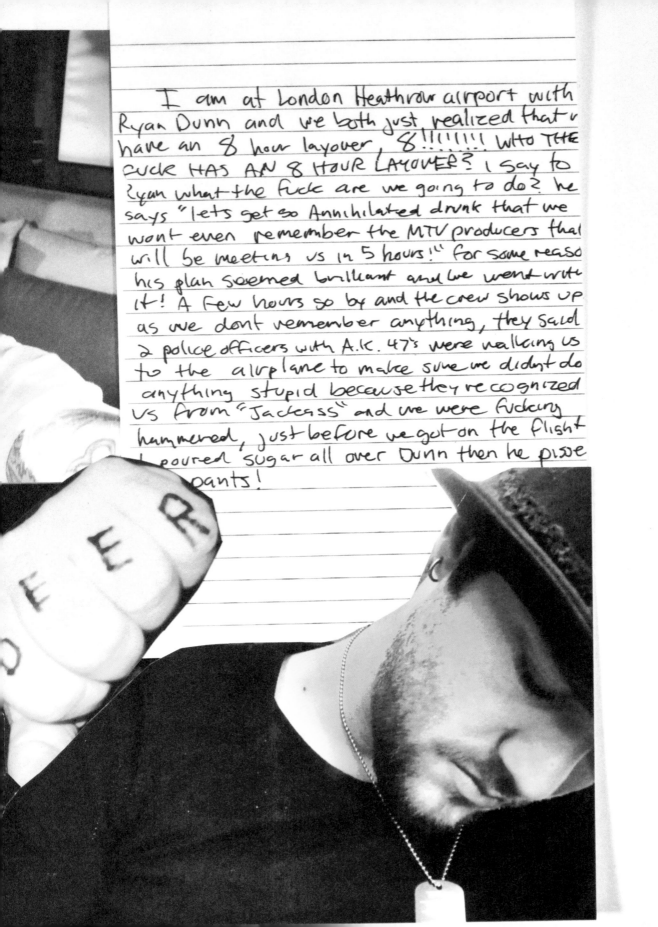

I am at London Heathrow airport with Ryan Dunn and we both just realized that v have an 8 hour layover, 8!!!!!!! WHO THE FUCK HAS AN 8 HOUR LAYOVER? I say to Ryan what the fuck are we going to do? he says "lets get so Annihilated drunk that we wont even remember the MTV producers that will be meeting us in 5 hours!" for some reaso his plan seemed brilliant and we went with it! A few hours go by and the crew shows up as we dont remember anything, they said 2 police officers with A.K. 47's were walking us to the airplane to make sure we didnt do anything stupid because they recognized us from "Jackass" and we were fucking hammered, just before we got on the flight I poured sugar all over Dunn then he pisse pants!

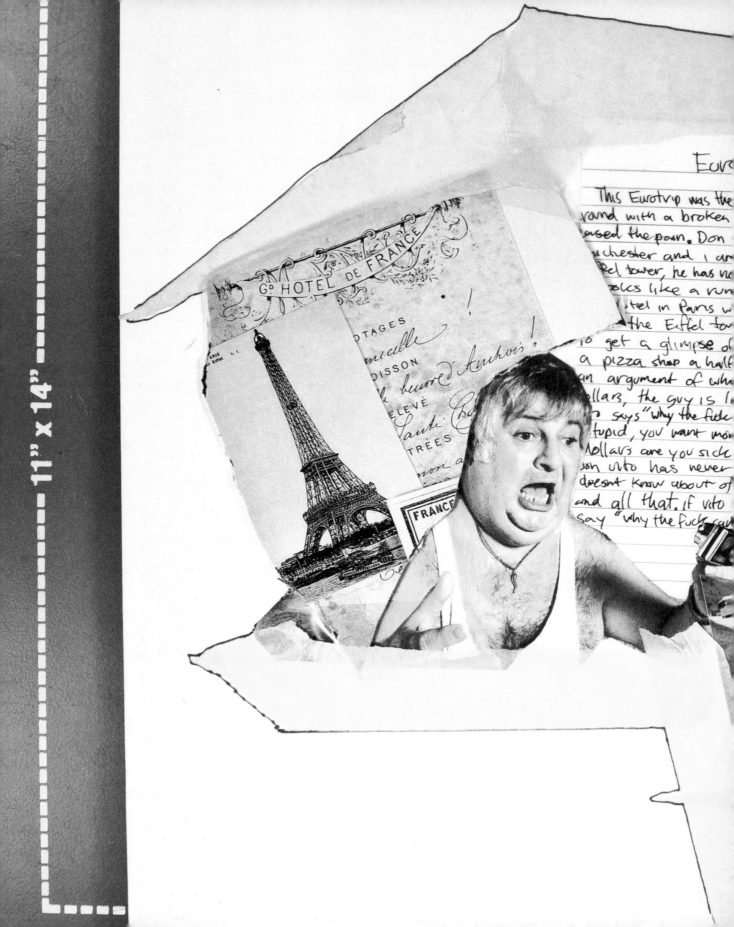

**11" x 14"**

Gd HOTEL DE FRANCE

FRANCE

...OTAGES
...micelle
...DISSON
...beurred Anchois!
...ELEVÉ
...aute
...TRÉES
...non a...

Eur...

This Eurotrip was the...
...round with a broken...
...eased the pain. Don...
...nchester and I am...
...fel tower, he has ne...
...ooks like a run...
...tel in Paris w...
...the Eiffel tow...
...o get a glimpse of...
...a pizza shop a half...
...an argument of wha...
...ollars, the guy is l...
...o says "why the fu...
...tupid, you want mo...
...ollars are you sick...
...on vito has never...
...doesn't know about of...
...and all that. if vito...
...say "why the fuck ca...

DAVOS, SWITZERLAND
10.05

Venice was a
because the entire
means if you have
ready to spend $50
taxi unless you wa
filled water! One m
plenty Johnny walter b
most nk I have e
tos of where

monaco is for st
own poodles and
is a police officer
left the dinner tal
lay down in my
over slam my
cuff me! They
have in monac
no reason
of the M
all came
me, I w
as a g
back

but very expensive
is underwater. wh
to go anywhere g
dollars on a water
wim in the shit
decided to drink
naking it the 2n
chece out
het night —

ich fucks who
Versace shit.
y block and I
to go outside and
fit. Then 2 cops com
inst the wall and hand
what buisness does a g
were roughing me up for on
houted loud enough for
members to hear and they
escued me. If they didn't he
ably be in a monaco prison
n no passport trying to get
erica!

**16" x 20"**

U.S.A.

FOR

will smith party
at armory in philly
Canada Day (CAN)

**6**
Hellzinki,
FINLAND
Film Viva la bam
w/Raab
New Moon ●

**7**
TALLIN
ESTONIA
w/Jussi from 69 eyes
we decided to do cdec on
the ferry, but it was accidently
speed, and we were up for
2 1/2 days!

**8**
RUISROCK w/
Turbonegro + HIM
went to villes house
+ drank karhu

flew
to
Philly

C needs seafood **13**
Jimmy Pops
saw Mr. and Mrs.
Smith w/missy

**14**

**15**
Edited HIM
Documentary
Turks head inn

Ocean,
MD

40cm x 50cm

Kick flip in Miami, I s
Probably more faggoty then R
Missy says J-see

The reason why this photo is yellow is
'cause Gees cat pissed all over it!

CKY
BAM MARGERA &
BRANDON DiCAMILLO

CKY
WITH 25 MINUTES
OF BONUS FOOTAGE

Jay-Z that night, i think hes a home-
contos. Hes officially the gayest!

red nice!

dfsskljd;;lkjaeorti;lkj;dflj;uperoti;
;sdfljjk sdkleiu x;ijfs dsfklixleoiu

My neighbors hated me the day I moved
into my new house. It probably has a lot
to do with the fact that slayer play
that night. Also i forgot to show up to
the welcome to the neighborhood par
Oops!

st of the ideas I come
with are more complicated
write down, so I will
st draw shitty pictures
d that is considered
y writers credit.
u can thank the red
e on the airplanes
r that!

Novak was willing to do whatever it took to be best man for the wedding, but technically Jess, my broth would have to be. But if Novak is willing to do anything then I should put it to the test. So I dared him to shave the top of his head off so he looks like a bald 70 year old. He did it without question. That nig we went to Kildares pub and he had a hat on so it was unnoticeable. He hit on some college chick and brought one back home and drank more beer by the time she made it to his room his hat came off and he forgot about his terrible hairde that causes low self esteem. He was eating her out and she looked up at him and screamed in desgust and put her clothes back on. He came out of his room unsatified and humiliated and drowned his sorrows in booze!

NoVaks sick ass HEMROID ASS

Just fun
Natalie bu
as a bet
nisht he
Forgot all
luck and
as eating

**ORIGINS: PIV**

...s radio show talking about how
...e top of his head like an old man
... best-man in the wedding. That
...o the bar with a hat on and
...t his hairdo. He met a college
... her back to the house. As he
...out his hat came off and
...table and disgusted. Novak was
... had low self esteem!

your best friend? tough
sh. i Guess that would all depend
on @ the dAte and time like a
fuckin Rolex, @ sometimes its Novak,
sometimes i want to cave his fucking face in,
I like dunn though medicine has made him
different. dice has always been the same
addicted to K-mart Ville when were around.
shit, maybe Philly if you'd think about
it. @ EUROPE 2004

2. fuck these motherfuckers who are
43% By Volume    who open up clothing lines
and sell the shit out with a 500ft
billbourd on sunset strip. and claim
the fame, lets face it. they HAD help
THEY HAD HELP! i Scarlett !!!
Johanson....
who gives a fuck

3. skateboarders huck themselves down
motherfucking Do stairs for Nothing!
Nothing!! fuckin Hell. Meanwhile jude
Law is getting 2-million dollars for memorize
27 lines in a shitty film. what happened to
the world. tiger woods hits golf balls for
millions and some motherfucker with nothy
is doing this — show stg trace! Pretending
in our Blood!
Jen
Rivell

og duty - *[illegible]*

Vowels in wood

in trees w/ se

. Go kart thro

. Dico Tattersall
London /tank

r "Burned alive by love" we
onths later In a castle ou
tury man" and my favorite

Powering out 10 music videos for cky II
a year I felt I had enough experience to
[vid]eo for my favorite band "HIM". I had
[figure]d out, I will fly out to Finland, get e[veryone]
[li]quored up and talk them into letting me dire[ct]
before they found out I was only 21! so a[bout]
[week]s went by and I got a message from the
["Va]lo" that we were going to be in LA at
[the same] time. They were mixing there album in studio[s]
I was in Hollywood filming jackass shit so I k[new]
a perfect opportunity and i didnt give a [fuck]
an advance from the record label. I said [I]
[I w]ill pay for the video and if you like it y[ou]
[keep i]t!" we shot the video for $77,000 at the [house]
[starrin]g Juliette lewis and the shit went # 1 a mon[th]
[in th]e UK. BMG suggested that I do the next 3 b[ut]
[I did]nt that. Note to self - taking a $77,000 risk wa[s]
worth every penny!"

the next vid[eo]
[o]f Prauge fo[r]
[one o]f all time" an[d]

# THE 69 EYES VIDEO SHOOT
# LOS ANGELES AND PHILADELPHIA

I am Flying to Los Angeles with th
69eyes to film a scene at the rainbow
room for the Lost boys. I can't help
to notice everyone loooking at us!! I thi...
its frcking hilarious! picture these dudes
prancing through the airport—

# LOST
# BOYS!

Not to mention the X-ray machine,
Jussi seriously took 25 minutes taking off h
punk rock Flare to get through the termin
the people behind him were so pissed! I hope
missed theyre flights! Ha!

TL0304    GA      GA0   22      COMP

EVENT CODE    SECTION/AISLE   ROW/BOX  SEAT    ADMISSION
$    0.00    STANDING ROOM            0.00
             ELECTRIC FACTORY PRESENTS
SECTION/AISLE
    GA          THE 69 EYES
TM    1X      AN ALL WEATHER EVENT
ROW    SEAT
GA0   22      THEATRE OF LIVING ARTS
TLA600C       334 SOUTH ST, PHILA.
4MAR06        SAT MAR 4, 2006 9:00PM

# CARVER CITY
## NEW ALBUM!!!!!

They took Hi- to the Dowtown
Dallas Jail for 12 hours miss
the show and the departures
the buses to Houston. I
to stay there to bail hi-
i show up to the jail a-
and they wouldnt rel
cause he is still too
I went back to the
waited till 8am for
on the hotel door. I
door naked lookin
with a bloody
girlfriend. The
Novak a ride
dropped me an
meet me.
Novaks 50
got on t
philly m-
definitel-
least
Fil

dear bam,
we have sirius radio on our tv and my son has been
listlen to your show. just recently i tuned in to the
show and and i have to say i was qiuet apalled in to the
an angry mother

HANOI RO

ite Partner &

Dead Beat Da-

I NEED A R

I'LL BE A JUN

IN FOUR YEARS

I like to draw pictures of my neighbors on buses

Going to hell!

I gave $20,000 to boarderline the local skatepark in westchester which is fucking pointless because when I go there I cant even break a sweat skating Cause every kid and soccer mom wants to talk, have an autograph or shoot a fucking photo and I dont mind it when im out, but NOT when I'm skating, So i dont go there anymore. I built a fucking massive ramp in my backyard to skate for $100,000 to the fdr hessians to build. Now the fucking township is trying to tear it down. because its a dangerous structure. No fucking shit! I will skate this ramp till they physically come in with the bare hands and remove it. FUCK THEM OLD HORSE POETRY LOVING FAGGOTS!

am
ump ↓

SERIOUS
AS
SHITWATER!

RGERa

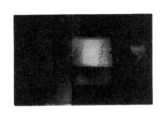

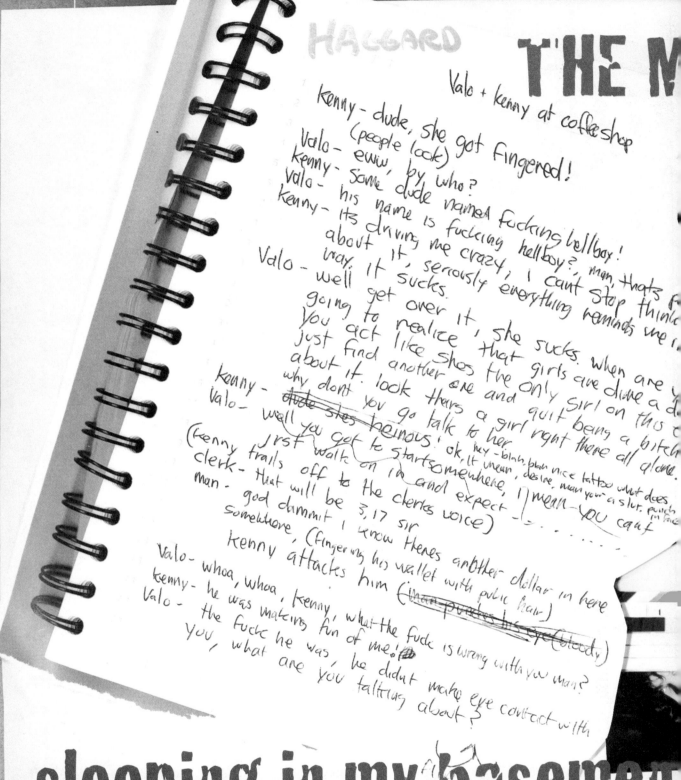

# KING OF HAGGARD '02

(4)

**luring a fake because**
**NG PROBlems**

Novak had a little too much fun.
Being naked and not getting kicked out for once he flew to the
show in orlando florida to join
the tour with me for good. I
wanted to make his existance
worthy by taking a shit in the
middle of the street, but his diet
consists of booze, pills and cocaine.
So he didnt have to shit till the
4th day of tour in Dallas Texas.
He says "Bam break out the camera I
have to shit." Of course I do and
He goes out into the middle of the
freeway and drops trou! He Now
Has a foot of shit hangin out of
His ass causing a great traffic
Jam. The 3rd car that passed him beeps
and flicked him off, the fourth car was
a police car! A fucking police car!!
worst timing ever, he couldnt even Hide.
They come out instantly hand cuffed
Him and walk up to me and say
"you think its fucking funny to
Film your pal shit in the middle
of the street" and i busted out
laughing and said "NO!"

Liquor and Poke

MAD LIBS
HOW TO SURVIVE
A SANDSTORM

CKY
www.cky-online.com

ALWAYS STRIKE A MATCH AWAY FROM YOU

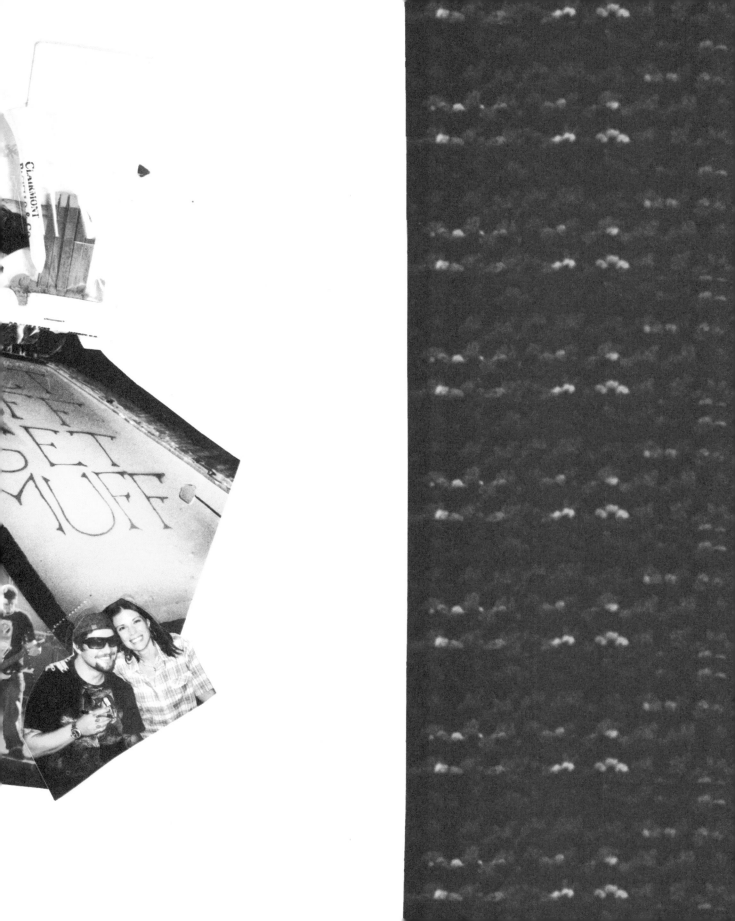

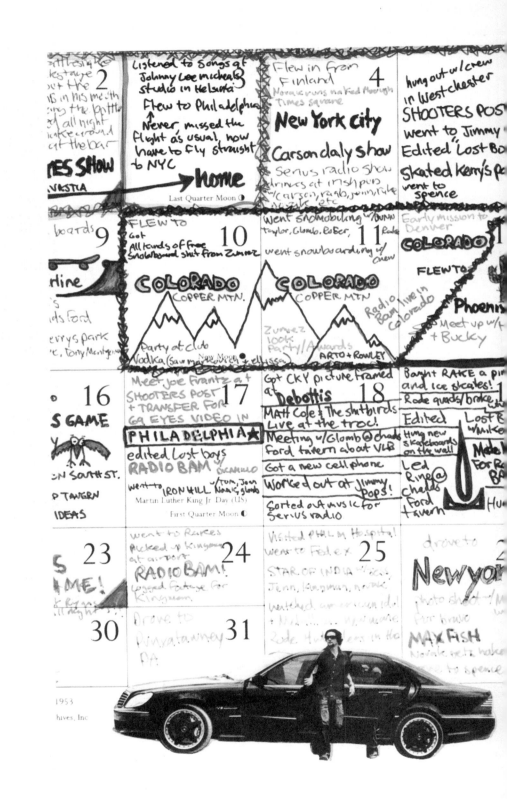

| | | | |
|---|---|---|---|
| ...at the stage out the 1B in his mouth ...ing the bottle ...d all night ...lake around at the bar **TES SHOW** ...VASTIA | **2** Listened to songs at Johnny Lee micheals studio in Helsuta. Flew to Philadelphia ↑ Never missed the flight as usual, now have to fly straight to NYC ➡️ **home** *Last Quarter Moon* ☽ | Flew in from Finland **4** Novak runs naked through Times square **New York City** **Carson daly show** Serius radio show drinks at irish pub w/carson, raab, jenn, rake Novak etc | hung out w/crew in Westchester **SHOOTERS POST** went to Jimmy Edited "Lost Bo... Skated Kerry's p... went to spence |
| ...boards **9** ...hine 's ...ds ford ...erry's park 'e, Tony Montgo... | **FLEW TO** Got **10** All kinds of Free snowboard shit from Zumiez **COLORADO** COPPER MTN. Party at Club Vodka (saw my... *New Moon* ● | Went snowmobiling w/Novak taylor, Glomb, Raab **11** Raab went snowboarding w/ crew Zumiez 100% party/Awards (Melissa) ARTO + ROWLEY | Early mission to Denver **COLORADO** FLEW TO **Phoenix** Meet up w/... + Bucky |
| o **16** **S GAME** y ...N SOUTH ST. P TAVERN IDEAS | Meet joe frantz at **17** SHOOTERS POST + TRANSFER FOR 69 EYES VIDEO IN **PHILADELPHIA ★** edited Lost boys **RADIO BAM** Di Camillo went to **IRON HILL** w/Tom, Joan Novak, Glomb *Martin Luther King Jr. Day (US)* *First Quarter Moon* ☽ | Got CKY picture framed at **Debottis** **18** Matt Cole & The shitbirds Live at the troc! Meeting w/Glomb @ chads ford tavern about VLB Got a new cell phone Worked out at Jimmy Pops! Sorted out music for Serius radio | Bought RAKE a pir... and ice skates! Rode quads/broke... Edited **Lost B...** Hung new while... skateboards on the wall Led Made ... Ring @ For Ra... chads BA... ford tavern Hu... |
| S **23** ...ME! k Ry... ...ll night... | went to Rakes **24** Picked up Kingsman at airport **RADIO BAM!** Logged footage for Kingsman. Drove to **30** Punxatawney **31** PA. | Visited Phil in Hospital! **25** Went to FEd. ex. STAR OF INDIA w/Jenn, Kingman, novak. watched american idol + Ned ... Made ... Rode 4 wheelers in the... | drove to **2...** **New yor...** photo shoot w/... for brave **MAX FISH** Novak gets baked ...to spence |
| 1953 hives, Inc | | | |

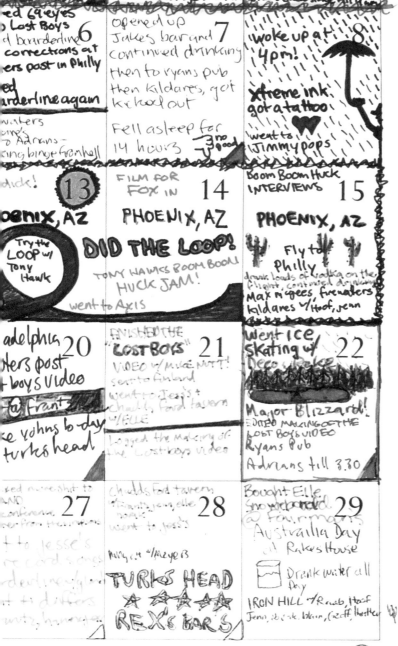

| | | |
|---|---|---|
| ed 69 eyes<br>o Lost Boys<br>d borderline **6**<br>corrections at<br>ers post in Philly<br>ed<br>rderline again<br>waters<br>mp's<br>o Adrians -<br>ing binge from hall | opened up **7**<br>Jakes bar and<br>continued drinking<br>then to ryans pub<br>then kildares, got<br>kicked out<br><br>Fell asleep for<br>14 hours ⇒ no good | I woke up at **8**<br>4pm!<br><br>Xtreme ink,<br>got a tattoo<br>♥<br>went to<br>Jimmypops |
| dick! ⑬<br>PHOENIX, AZ<br>Try the<br>LOOP w/<br>Tony<br>Hawk<br>went to Axis | FILM FOR **14**<br>FOX IN<br>PHOENIX, AZ<br>**DID THE LOOP!**<br>TONY HAWKS BOOM BOOM<br>HUCK JAM! | Boom Boom Huck **15**<br>INTERVIEWS<br>PHOENIX, AZ<br>Fly to<br>Philly<br>drank loads of vodka on the<br>flight, continued drinking<br>Max n gees, firewaters<br>kildares w/ Hoof, Jenn |
| adelphia **20**<br>ters post<br>+ boys video<br>@ Frant<br>ke Johns b day<br>turks head | FINISHED THE **21**<br>"LOST BOYS"<br>VIDEO w/ MIKE MITT!<br>sent to Finland<br>went to Jess's +<br>chadds ford tavern<br>w/ ELLE<br>Logged the making of<br>the "Lost boys" video | Went ICE **22**<br>Skating w/<br>Deco + Blake<br><br>Major Blizzard!<br>EDITED MAKING OF THE<br>LOST BOYS VIDEO<br>Ryans Pub<br>Adrians till 3:30 |
| ed nine shit to **27**<br>AND<br>continued<br>ee from the union<br>+ to Jesse's<br>e card songs<br>borderline w/<br>t to d others<br>unts, homies, | chadds ford tavern **28**<br>+ taverns, jenn, elle<br>deco<br>went to jess's<br>nothing on w/ meyeB<br>**TURKS HEAD**<br>★ ★ ★ ★ ★<br>**REX's BAR's** | Bought Elle **29**<br>snowboard<br>@ Fourman's<br>Australia Day<br>at Rakes House<br>🥛 Drank water all<br>Day<br>IRON HILL w/ Raab, Hoof<br>Jenn, sbink, blain, Geoff, Heather |

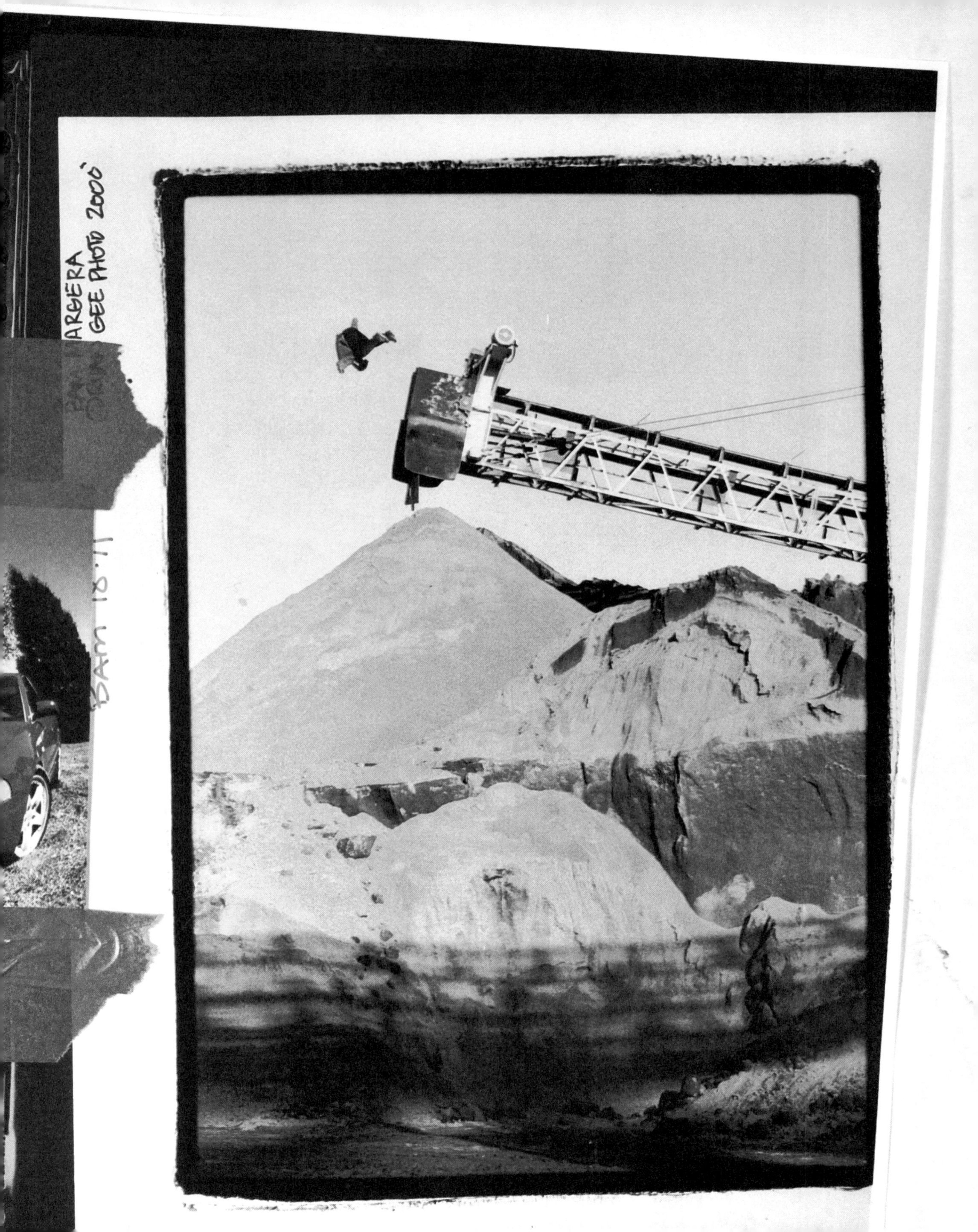
ARGERA
GEE PHOTO 2000
BAM 18'11

14 Ryan Errands!
skated
**FDR**
hangout w/ Vito

15 SHIT GOOSE! 4 wheel version at the pine Barrens in New Jersey! went to Jimmy pops warehouse

16 Got 6 pictures framed at deaths in west chester skated empty pool in PA
wentz 15N 4/use Cross

17 ● flew to **HOLLYWOOD**
71 restaurant galleries "/ Terry

21 skated sat
taken time to Philly w/ the guys
Hung out with Hillary Duff Jr
Philly Vibe
Turks head inn

22 built ramp into the pool!
skate photos!
skated backyard live w/ mike maldonado
got a shower!!
Naked chicks in pool!

23 film Rockstars episode!
Jimm is a French & too far away man!
BLOODHOUND GANGS FIRST SHOW

24 FILMED ROCKSTAR EPISODE
tv show

SO ... I BOUGHT 8 CARS @ $800 BUCKS A PIECE JUST T[...]
HOW FAR THEY GO. SO ON THIS ONE, IT HAPPEND TO B[...]
BACKSIDE SMITH MOTHER FUCKER!!!

BRICKS ON THE GAS PEDALS TO SEE

SKATE TRICK, AND THAT SHIT IS A

RNSWALLOWERS!

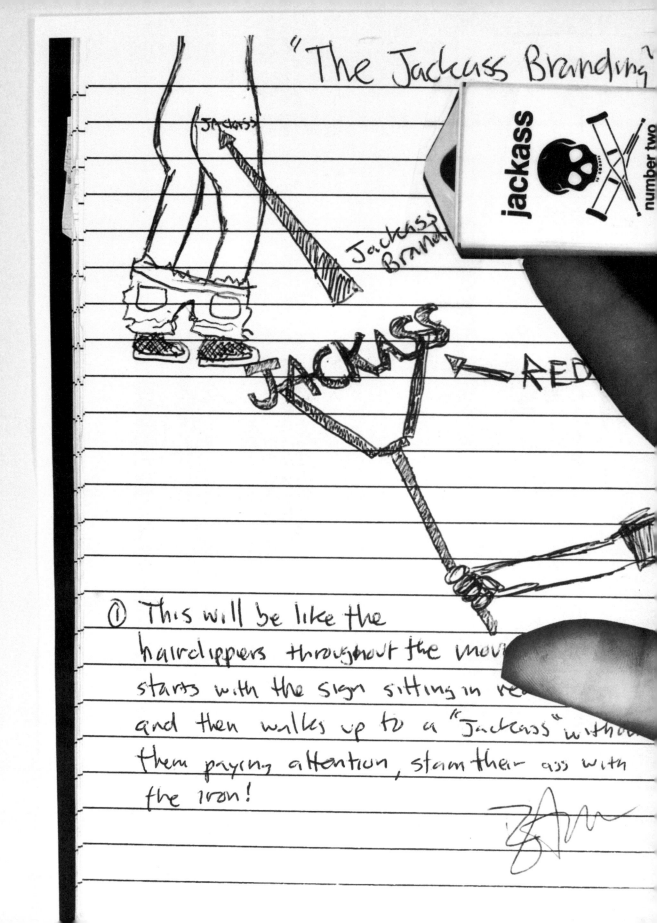

"The Jackass Branding"

① This will be like the
hairclippers throughout the mov[ie]
starts with the sign sitting in rea[...]
and then walks up to a "Jackass" witho[ut]
them paying attention, stam their ass with
the iron!

strong Ass man competition

→ cup test

← Naked of course

HIT ME

OH!

WELCOME!

object of game hit cock as hard as make the bell ring!

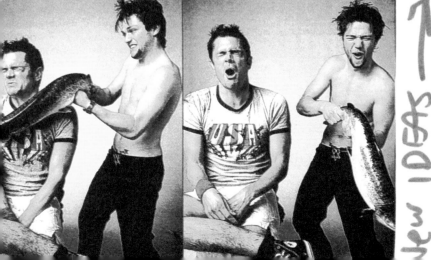

New IDEAS

SUNDAY

**LOGGED HIM TAPES**
**TILL 3pm** 3
drove Lambo w/shitpose
Got Haircut
**EDITED HIM DOC.**

Duffers II
Daylight Saving Time begins

drank
Booze
Novak did
a naked piss
to Fakie
Radio Bam

Skated the
Driveway

Cops come over
thanks to Jenn 10
and me! (Bam)

Slept
the day
away

Filmed vids
for cky challenge 11
went to Jess's in lambo
Mitch's gym
**RADIO BAM**
Mitch's gym again
HOOTERS

12
NEW. YORK
TRL
autograph sig.
Virgin megastore.

17
Fly to
California

18
Jackass
Commentary
went to Roxy w/bmy
+ Jessica simpson

19
Jackass
Commentary

24

25

2

EDITED @ Dakota
VH1 interview 1

HIM
MANSION!

April Fool's Day
Last Quarter Moon ◗

LOS ANGEL
TO PHILADE

LOGGED HIM F
MITCH'S G

FAIR
ELEMENT
AUTOGR
SIGNI

GOT ANNIHL
KILDARES
pooltable

NEW
TURBONE
sk8
FDR

Goosecr
visited jess
Hooters, 15

ne barrens
New Jersey

Shoot w/
mark weiss 7

meeting w/ cartoon
people at kildares

RVIEW w/ BRAVO

Skated the driveway 8

Billy Idol in
Philadelphia

Manaysunk w/ Jimmy Pop
New Moon ●

film
HIM

20

*life is a flying leap*

27

always told my self when I turn 21 I wont be that
that goes straight to the bar, sure enough my 21s
day I was at 15 north Hammering down shots! Ive wasted man
nights at the bar talking to randoms about absolutely noth
thinking it was so cool getting recognized by Hot chicks. I w
ould have rewound life and skated 50% of my alchohol consu
ed. Dont get me wrong Im all for getting shitfaced, but when
do it everynight for 2 years you got to take a step b
chill. The problem with me is that I could never say :
only drink on special occasions because everynight is a
cial occasion. One night I will be at kildares with the C
, then to the troc for a children of bodom show, then to LA
Sean Penn and John Cusack on the beach. Every fucking
is a special occasion, thats the problem. But
least its a good Problem.

Raab got expelled from East high school for shitting on a locker which gave me the brilliar idea to quit! I already knew what I wanted to do in life which was skateboarding. I had to listen to my guidence counslor tell me I am making a terrible desici because skateboarding is a fad and it will dissape in 2 years, then he started rambling on about a student similar to me quit to become a famous rap and he saw him 2 years later working at Mcdona All the shit he said was in one ear and out the other, I felt I was good enough to be a profession skater and I was willing to fly to california to f out. Then theres always the infamous question teachers, relatives and your girlfriends parents as "what happens if you break your neck? then what?"
then I say " I will wait for my neck to heal then I would try the same trick again"

And they all look at you like youre a fucking idiot. Fuck it - theres no way im being misera! like all of you people working a 9 to 5 everyday.

I will take my chances!

**10K Barb-Q**

Have a barbeque on a wooden deck with your friends and cook marsh till it breaks off!

# Like it or not 'Jackass' is

## REVIEW

**By BETSY PICKLE**
Scripps Howard News Service

No one can say that the guys in "Jackass: Number Two" don't suffer for their art. Well, aside from those who would argue that there's nothing in the sequel to the 2002 hit that resembles art at all.

Art or not, the bawdy, earthy, puerile humor of "Jackass: Number Two" is definitely entertaining, and it's probably more sadistic than its forebear: Romans fed Christians to the lions at the Colosseum. Johnny Knoxville, Bam Margera, Steve-O, Chris Pontius, Jason "Wee Man" Acuña, Ryan Dunn, Dave England, Ehren McGhehey convene in "Jackass: Number Two and...

jackass
number two

WARNING: The stunts in this movie were performed by professionals, so neither you nor your dumb little buddies should attempt anything from this movie.

OR→

**ck**

...om & Jerry"
...ndfolding
...ubjecting
...yak's caresses.
...ence has a
...ulls keeping an
...argera as he
...is buttocks to be
...d.

...er animals contribut-
...o the pain and suffer-
...include sharks, ana-
...das, a king cobra, a
...ech, bees and a stallion.

The group's fascination
with bodily emissions hits
its peak (or nadir) with
the stallion. It's the one
part of the film that
requires a black censoring
bar.

What makes all this
watchable is the gleeful
attitude and friendship o...
the men, and the fact tha...
even the most disgusting
antics are amusing,
whether in a "laughing a...
with them" or "laughing a...
them" spirit.

There's no order to the
antics, and Tremaine
could have done a better
job of editing some of the...
weaker material and orga...
nizing more of a build. A...
95 minutes, the film
should never drag, but it
does a couple of times.

Rated R for extremely
crude and dangerous
stunts, sexual content,
nudity and language.

...m
...s
...Jason
...Preston
...l and
...recon-
...or Jeff
...umber
...e first film
...of-the-millen-
...how that
...excrement,
...nd an obsession
...ring the male
...abound in "Two."
...lm starts, hilari-
...with the running of
...lls – through a sub-
...n neighborhood, with
...huffing, overgrown
...s barely staying ahead
...them. Later, Knoxville

## SHIT DOLLAR

## BAMS SHIT

~~We~~ put a $10 right out front of a supermarket with shit underneath and film whet idiot picks it up. Bam & Bam come out of nowhere in nice suits like News reporters. with a mic and the whole deal. "Congradulations you are the winner of the shit dollar, how do you feel? are you gonna buy a lot of shit with that dollar sir? give him a ghetto trophy.

115

To think, 10 minutes
after this photo was
taken Knoxville was in
the hospital for a
concusion cause dunn
drove over a Mountain
Lion!

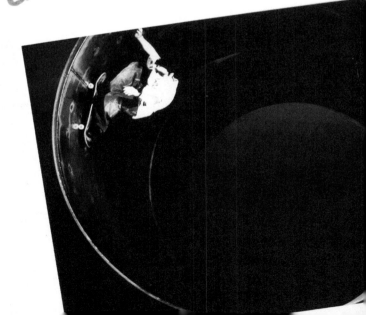

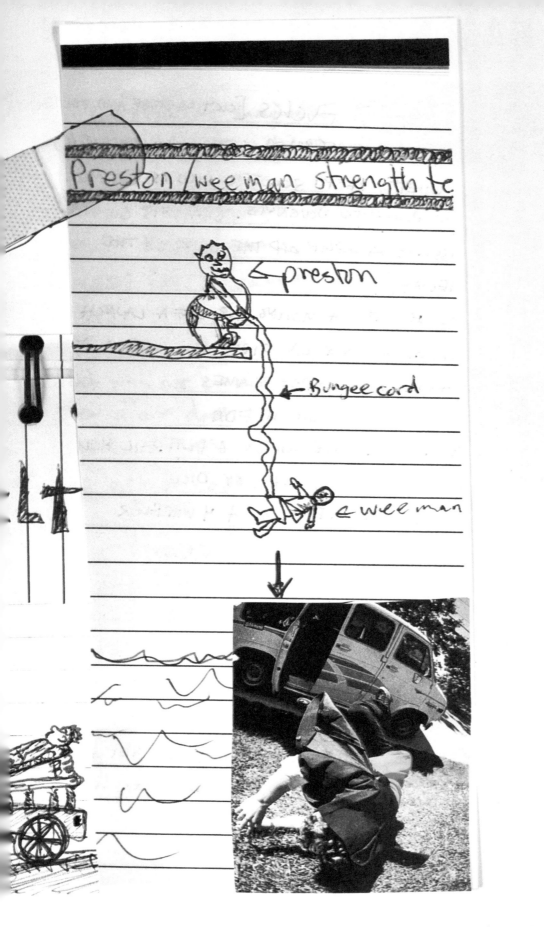

Preston/weeman strength te

← preston

← Bungee cord

← weeman

ME AND KNOXVILLE FUCKING
AROUND ON BIKES AT THE
PARAMOUNT LOT 2 WEEKS
BEFORE HE FUCKED HIS
DICK UP TRYING TO BACK
FLIP ON A DIRT BIKE ..

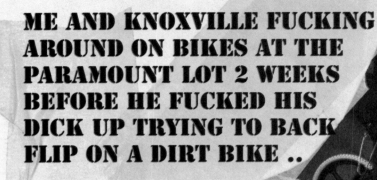

MISSY & MYSELF
KISSING MAJA OF
THE SOUNDS BEFORE
HER SHOW AT THE
PALLADIUM .....

IGGY AND I DRUNK AT A M

SUNSET MARQUIS MISSION

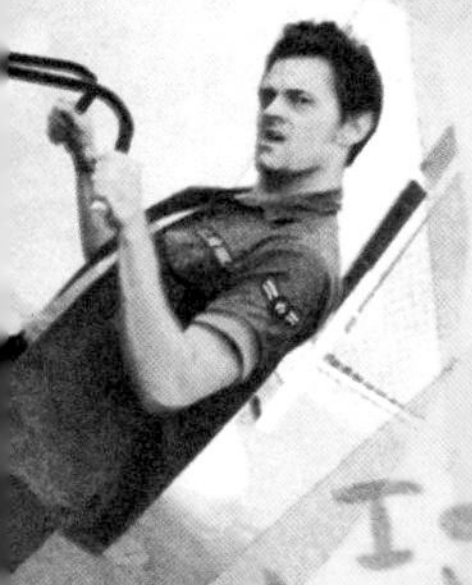

I ggy Pop
plays the wedding
Now im fuckin
freinds with him and
will meet him with
some booze before
one of his shows!
Fuck you if you have
something to
say!

LOS ANGELES 08

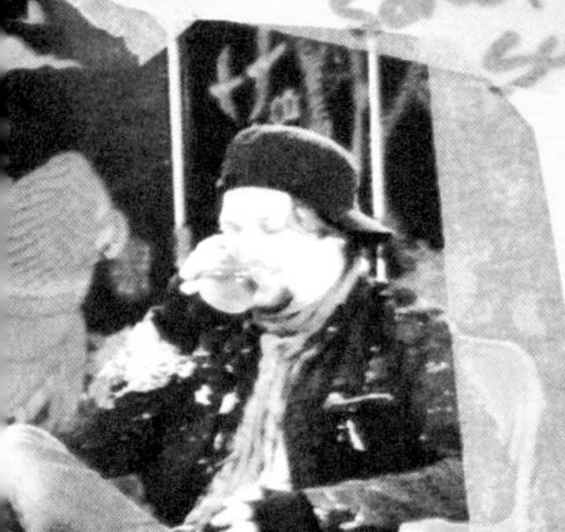

E INTERVIEW

40cm x 50cm

BAM MARGERA • TRICK TIPS • JASON DILL

**411 BAM.**

PARENTAL ADVISORY EXPLICIT CONTENT

**FREE BAM** BONUS DVD!

**the bam issue**
profile, road trip, spot check, and more

**jason dill** day in the life

**hot wheels** arms on fire

**61**

411 video magazine    skateboarding

'2005

May there be silly nights like this one

live late lasting laughs

2005

200

Begin filming HIM's Making of the album PO SIRE!

**28**

**FLY TO Finland**

DRINKS AT THE SCANDIC w/ 69 eyes, Burton, Muge, Ville, Jonna, Gas, etc

**29**

Hellzinki, **FINLAND**

FILMED 16mm w/ crater at TORNI

Lost and Found w/ville, Jean Jonna Mige, + The 69 eyes

H F

Drin CIGAR BAR LOST JOHN Edit VIDEO skate Color Shoot Skate Boo

listened to songs at Johnny Lee micheals studio in Helsinki

Flew to Philadelphia
↑ Never missed the flight as usual have w to NYC

**2**
6 in his mouth ing the bottle d all night cake crowd at the bar

**ES SHOW**

VRSTLA

Flew in from Finland **4**
Norais runs naked through Times square

**New York City**

daly show

hung out w/crew in Westchester **5**
SHOOTERS POST
went to Jimmy Pops
Edited "Lost Boys"

boards **9**

**COL**

tine

s ford

rrys park
e, Tony Montgom

Party
Vodka (s

Meet J
SHOOTE
+ TRAN
69 EY

**16**

S GAME
y O

**PHIL**

FLEW Y
Got
All kinds o
Snolaboa

**HOBBIT HOLE**

# JANUARY

| | FRIDAY | SATURDAY |
|---|---|---|
| RATTLESNAKE BOOZE | | Kabuki restaurant 1 |
| | Hellzinki, **FINLAND** woke up at 2pm **HIM SHOW** At TAVASTIA KLUB Drink Backstage till 4am | Hellzinki, **FINLAND** **HIM SHOW** At TAVASTIA KLUB Drink Backstage till 4am |
| 6 ons at Philly again | Opened up 7 Jakes bar and continued drinking then to ryans pub then kildares, got kicked out Fell asleep for 14 hours 3 no good | woke up at 8 4pm! Xtreme ink got a tattoo went to Jimmy pops |
| Granholl | | |

MAD HOUS

img168.tif

img169.tif

img170.tif

img171.tif

img172.tif

img173.tif

img174.tif

img175.tif

img178.tif

img179.tif

img180.tif

img183.tif

img184.tif

Deco in Texas 'o

img185.tif

img188.tif

img189.tif

img190.tif

img191.tif

img192.tif

img193.tif

img194.tif

img195.tif

img196.tif

img197.tif

img107.tif

img108.tif

**Bamboozled!**

img109.tif

gay fags is the funniest skit I think I have ever
filmed, as far as im concern, this is my best
work, 2 fags on rollerblade humping each other
damn brilliant!

img110.tif

img111.tif

img114.tif

img115.tif

img116.tif

img119.tif

img120.tif

img121.tif

img124.tif

img125.tif

img126.tif

img127.tif

img128.tif

img129.tif

img130.tif

img131.tif

img132.tif

img133.tif

img134.tif

img135.tif

img137.tif

phil drove this piece of shit
for 3½ years, there was a hole in the floor
and exaust leaked up in the car for us to breathe, this car is
to blame as of why I am so tweaked!

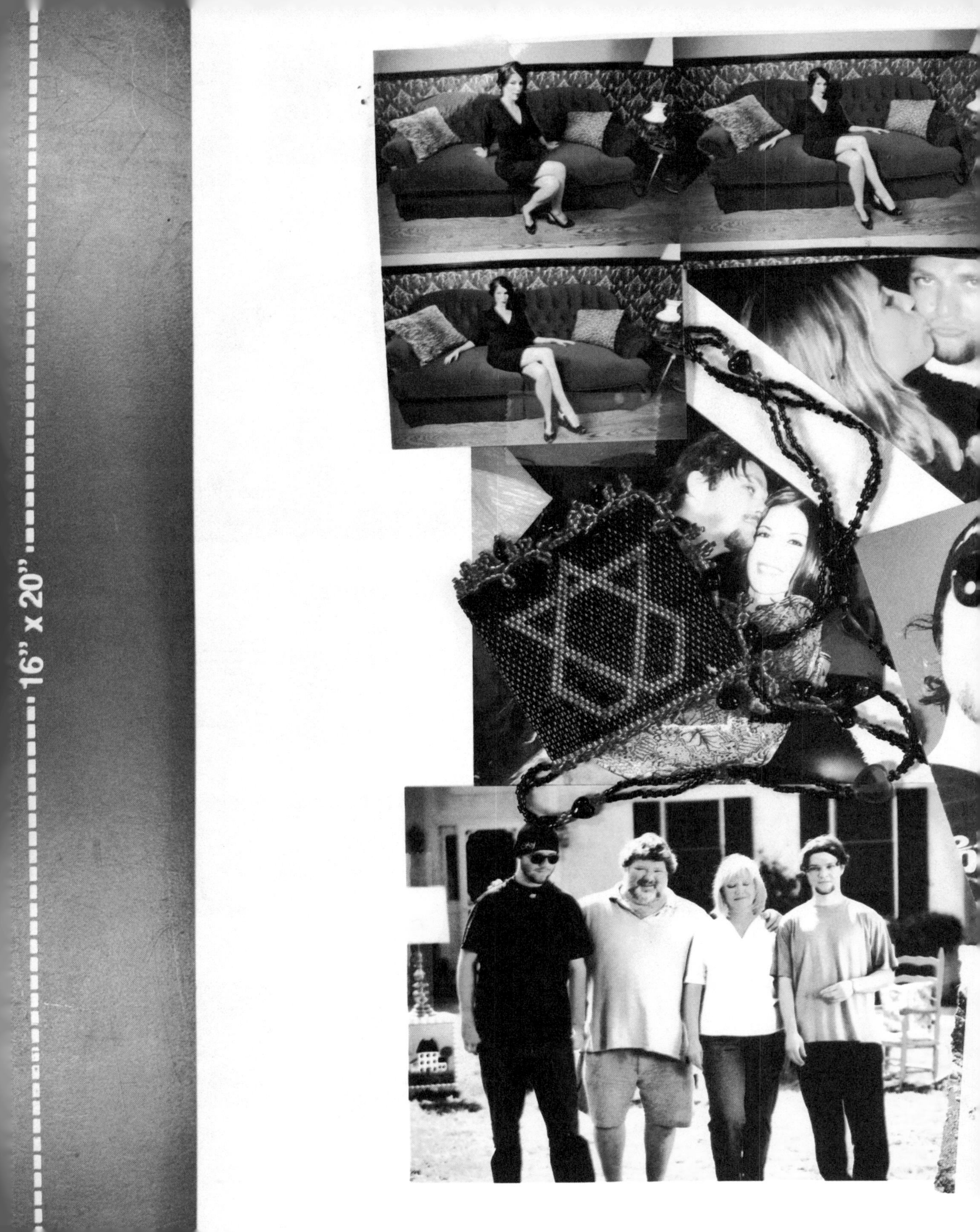
16" x 20"

Take your beer
See who your ab...
Sex with !

Have A !@%$# Day.
Mike Vallely

DANG!

of and
have

ree with the
ngel!

133

on Friday in Louisville, Ky.
up

Staff photo by Tom Kelly IV

for a protection from abuse
er Rivell. Margera claims Ri-
ence a few weeks ago.

# Margera files for protection

**By BRIAN FANELLI**
Staff Writer

WEST CHESTER – The on-
going turmoil between local
celebrity Brandon "Bam"
Margera and his ex-girl-
friend, Jennifer Rivell, con-
tinued on Friday, as Margera
appeared in a Chester
County Common Pleas Court
for a protection from abuse
(PFA) hearing, after Rivell al-
legedly broke into his Pocop-
son residence a few week
ago.

Margera, who urned

September, appeared be
Common Pleas Court Ju
Paula Francisco Ott dres
in black boots splatte
with white paint, a black
coat and black pants. A
waited to take the stand
held the hand of his fiar
Missy Rothstein.

The star of MTV's "Viv
Bam" and "Jackass" test
that Rivell, 33, climbed
wall surrounding his
idence, entered the
and kicked in a
or on Oct. 17.

RGERA, Pag

## INSIDE TODAY

Ellis
siness                B1
canester County       A3
nd gasified           D1
glaics pu             B4,5
                      A4
                      A2
                      B3
                      A5
                      C1
                      B3
                      B6

The Rubinstein's of
store's branch in Ken
re celebrates 25 year
ness. The store has
three locations in its
century of business.

**See Br**

ss the Penns
lastic Athletic
ross country me
Area runners
al threats.

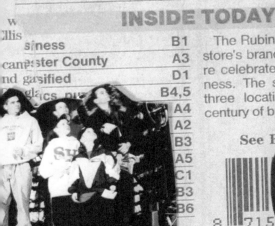

8  715

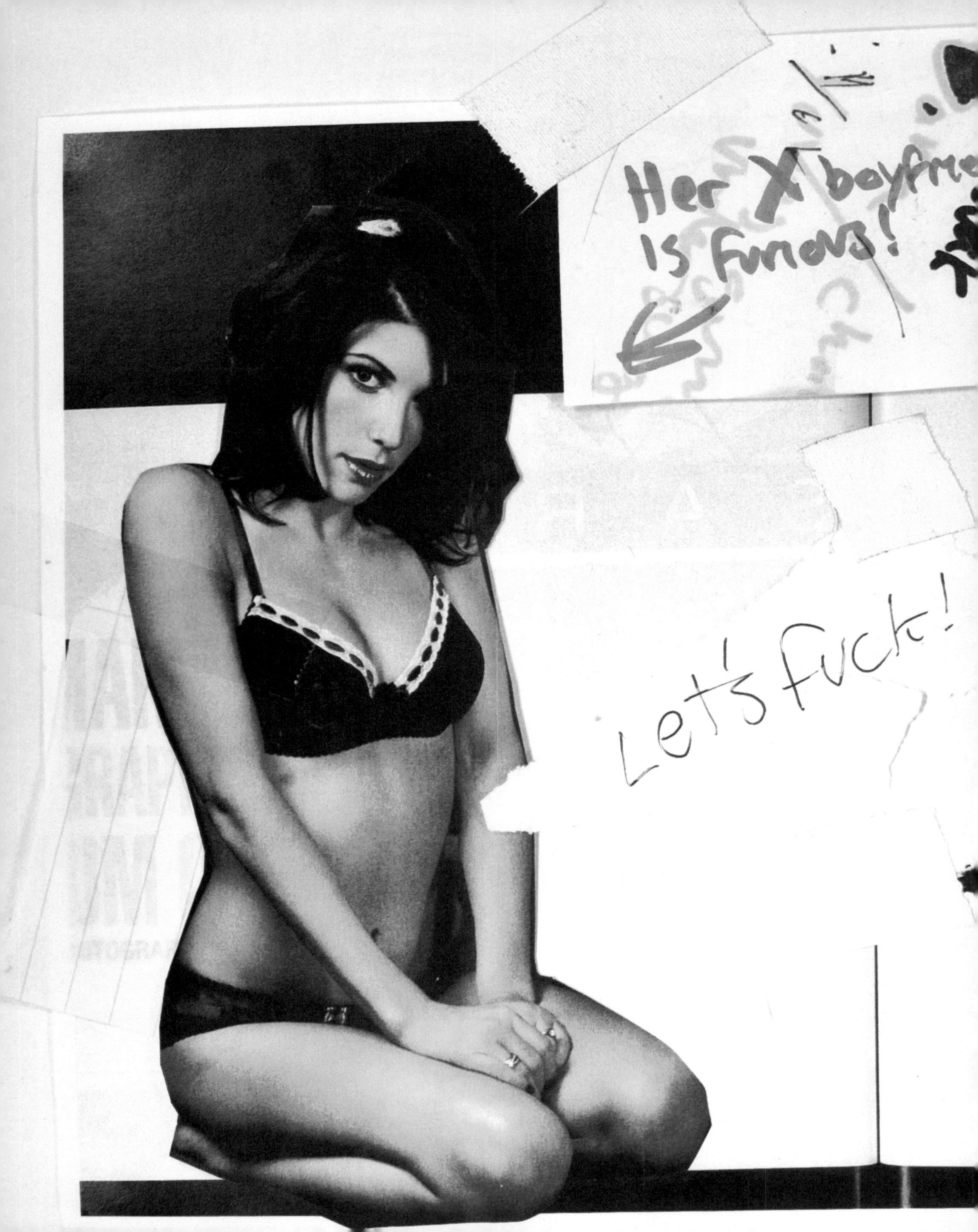

Her X boyfrie
is Furious!
Let's fuck!

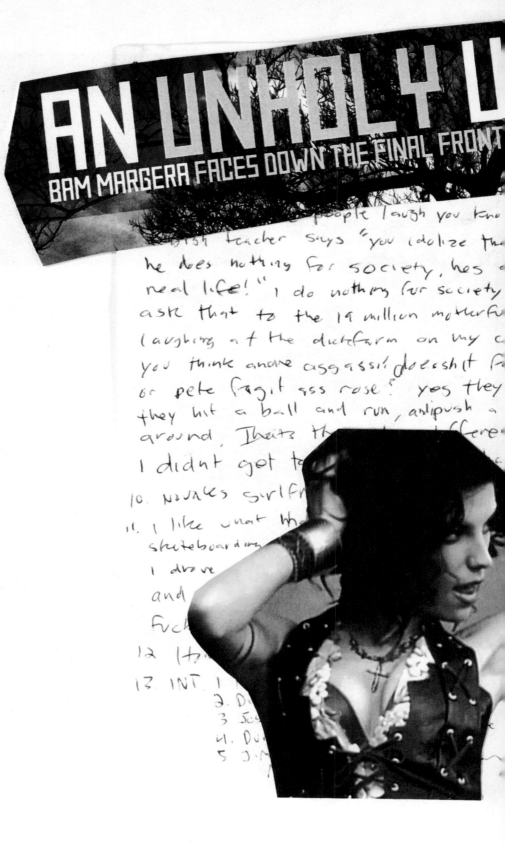

# AN UNHOLY U
## BAM MARGERA FACES DOWN THE FINAL FRONT

people laugh you kno
...lish teacher says "you idolize tha
he does nothing for society, hes a
real life!" I do nothing for society
ask that to the 19 million motherfu
laughing at the duckfarm on my c
you think andre aggassi doesshit fo
or pete fagit ass rose? yes they
they hit a ball and run, anlpush a
around. Thats the... ...fferen
I didnt get to

10. Novaks girlfr
11. I like what th
skateboarding
I drove
and
fuck

12. It...
13. INT. 1
2. Du
3. Sce
4. Du
5. J.M

stupid ass
kass!?
cess in
dont you
on the floor
git!
society?
tain?
of wood
t least
fane ahhh

d on

Both!!!
Put it
on paper

■ It's a cold morning in early January in West Chester, Pa. Bam Margera and a film crew are outside a cigar shop, filming scenes for his new MTV reality show, *Bam's Unholy Union*, which follows the exploits of the Jackass star and his bride-to-be, Melissa "Missy" Rothstein as they prepare to join in wedded bliss.

# DUBAI

Just Landed in Dubai after a draining 17 hour flight. Now I don't know why they chose us to pick on but missy and I both had to strip nude and checked our asses for drugs. I know perez hilton put a photo of us on the website that we were coming here for a honeymoon, and that music producer just got in big trouble for having coke on him. so they said "don't bring any drugs" Haha. So maybe that. Or the fact that we said we were married which is true. But it said Rothstien and Magera.

Sooo a mystery

Meanwhile im wearing a rosary and missy is a jew. They must have just thought we were up to no good. So 3hrs later of total bullshit. Missy is ready to fly home and I made her power it out to the resort. Once we got there it was totally true. We officially got fucked with!

I Toll ___ I Frenched her, but I Fucke

BAMS HOC

r !

| | 7 | 8 | 9 | 10 | 11 | 12 | 13 |
| 14 | 15 | 16 | 17 | 18 | 19 | 20 |
| 21 | 22 | 23 | 24 | 25 | 26 | 27 |
| | 29 | 30 | 31 | | | |

300 sit ups
Kickflip peppermill **4**

Went to Bloodhound
Gang Barb-a

New Hope ✝

Saw the USED in Wilmington
Party @ my house w/used
and Jared Leto

Drove to Wilmington for
Skug spots **11**

King of prussia mall
Look for skatespots
300 sit ups
saw
Billy IDOL in A.C.
stayed at
Grandparents' Day (US)
Missy's treehouse 2LNS
First Quarter Moon ◐

300 SIT UPS

INTERVIEWS **18**
w/MTva

TONY HAWK DEMO
ATHENS,
GEORGIA!

DINNER @ TRANSMETRO
DRIVE TO ATLANTA w/marv

**25**

LA

ZEIT

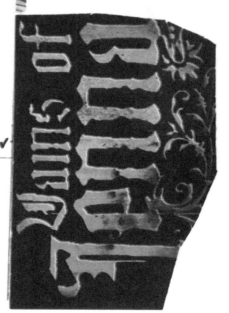

I drink beer
missy doesnt d
weed which is t
why the fuck do
X-gulfrien was e
fun, but afte
in flames, N
presentes attra

I knew this bitch was the one

Hockey kicks ass. Bam and Brandon. Above, Phil and Bam.

MISSY B-DAY at Rock 'n Ring
                    unkm/Beatsteaks
HOTEL DE ROME      Billy Talent
   BERLIN          Monday

1. Drink w/ panda cow
2. The search for duscon mandlik
3. Missy X flips out / caught on film
   servailence freaks out. we arr
   him
4. Antique car
5. Novak winds up in jail
6. cart for 6 tickets
7. get in shape to kick 2's
8. element creative meetings
9. designing adio shoes
10. meeting carte for New shit
11. skate at tony hawkes
    see the grand canyon
12. Jessicas shit in the pool.

during INT.

outdo yourself, do
No Like jackass
beat that but
and did what
ten times better.

stop break glass on wedding phone

burn sledge hammer your door in?)
juice,
Noose hung!
we save money!
400,000 gone, 5,000 left
back! Just do it! ✓
=Missy / who is your favorite Band?

"I feel like im watching a porno,
only im in it"

# For once, lea

**W**est Chester, most proud county seat for Chester County has a juicy role — well, the borough's a full-fledged costar — in *Bam's Unholy Union*, an MTV reality series that will chronicle the no-doubt-arduous yet butterflies-in-the-tummy-thrilling preparations for the wedding of East High School drop-out and proud *Jackass* jackass **Bam Margera**, 27, and childhood sweetie **Missy Rothstein**, 26. (The show was to debut last night.)

Bam and Missy, who appeared on **Howard**

# s not a stunt

**Stern**'s Sirius show yesterday, say they're totally ready to keep married life as adventurous as possible by developing a technique to, um, consummate their holy bond while *driving*. (Missy conceded the couple's Hummer has wide seats.)

Radar Online reports that Bam, whose latest sub-Mensa movie, *Jackass Number Two*, has grossed $84.5 mil, won't sell out his roots to move to New York or Lalaland. "Everything I need is in Pennsylvania," he tells the New York Daily News. Rock on, oard Dude!

The day before the wed...
the new ramp with To...
death gap for the firs...
it and try forcing m...
barges it after a heavy...
in the middle and br...
dipshit gets rushed to t...
Perscription to Percocettes.
Wheel chair going dow...
20 that day. 20! then...
days later and star...

had a hesh sesh on
We were trying the
Tony and I both make
be the third. He
boozing and jumps off
oth of his feet. The
all gets 2 casts and a
in the wedding in a
sle pilled up. He ate all
t to baltimore a few
ooting heroin again!

# Bam & Missy
## TIE THE KNOT!

*Jackass* star and pro-skater **Brandon "Bam" Margera**, 27, and graphic designer Melissa "Missy" Rothstein, 26, married before 350 guests including skating legend **Tony Hawk** and rocker **Iggy Pop** in Philadelphia on Feb. 3! The wedding, which aired April 3 on MTV's *Bam's Unholy Union*, capped off a madcap romance: The couple may have known each other since the sixth grade but only started dating two years ago. Last year, Bam popped the question outside of Cartier at the King of Prussia Mall in Pennsylvania. "Missy's totally down with Bam's craziness and supports him," MTV spokesman Travis Hicks tells *Star*. "They always seem like th...

PPEL ★

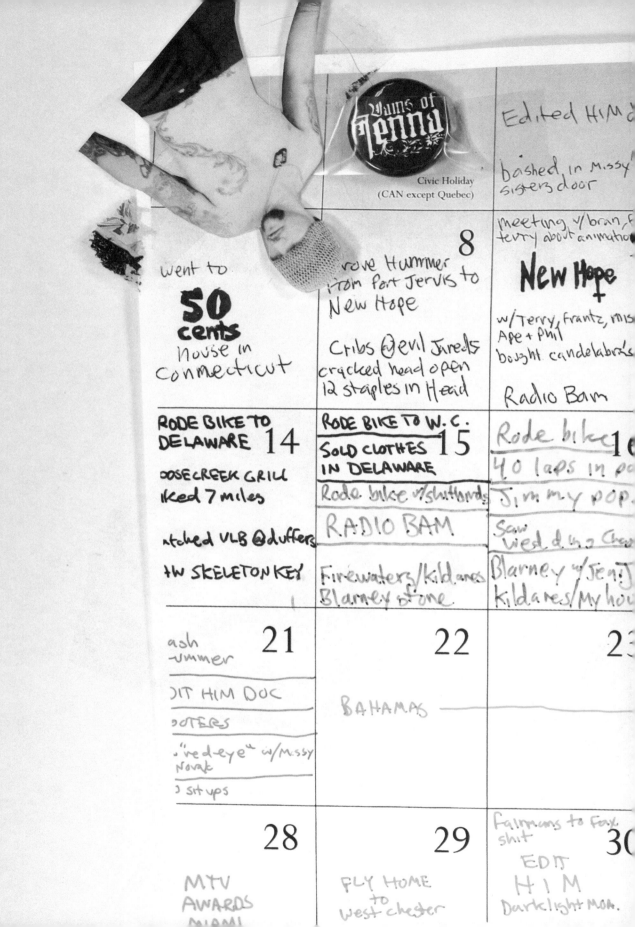

**Civic Holiday**
(CAN except Quebec)

Edited HIM

bashed in missy' sisters door

meeting w/ bran, terry about animation

went to

**50 cents** house in connecticut

rove Hummer from Port Jervis to New Hope **8**

Cribs @ evil Jareds cracked head open 12 staples in Head

**New Hope**

w/ Terry, frantz, mis Ape + Phil bought candelabra's

Radio Bam

RODE BIKE TO DELAWARE **14**

DOSE CREEK GRILL liked 7 miles

ntched VLB @ duffers

+W SKELETON KEY

RODE BIKE TO W.C. **15**
SOLD CLOTHES IN DELAWARE

Rode bike w/shutlands

RADIO BAM

Firewaters/ Kildares Blarney stone

Rode bike **16**

40 laps in po

Jimmy pop

Saw wed d in a Chees

Blarney w/ Jen J kildares/My hou

ash ummer **21**

DIT HIM DOC

OOTERS

"red eye" w/missy Novak

sit ups

**22**

BAHAMAS

**23**

**28**

MTV AWARDS

**29**

FLY HOME to west chester

fairmans to Fox shit **30**

EDIT HIM

Darklight MOA

| | | | |
|---|---|---|---|
| | Mantaloaking NJ for warnerbros Meeting at beach Novak liks oz's ass **New Moon** ● | went to west chester Kooma | Went to Eminem, cent + Lil J concert @ tweeter |
| nted HIM doc ched ty shame + sideways | | | |
| **10** rvers licsence center - Rims put an Hummer t w/ frantz + dico sildanes KED TO DELAWARE | **11** Took lambo to kerbek w/ Hann + Missy Rode bike 8 miles Met up w/ Meyers, Hoof + gary at Kooma | **12** Bought haloween shit in paoli Saw **MY chemical ROMANCE** ⅓ Avenged Sevenfold **First Quarter Moon** ◗ | **1** Cleaned radio room Biked 10 miles Party w/ shitbir went to Eminem w/ Lil Jon IRON HILL w/h mis |
| **17** UN HILL ODECRBEK Missy sit-ups | **18** Dust bowl! w/ SHITGOOSE 20 laps Rode bike 10 miles | **19** Biked 15 miles 200 situps got staples taken out 100 situps rderline party | **20** swimming kdw w/ Noak shoot skate Photo w/ gee saw brothers situps **27** |
| sit u mans te dr ger, G | | | |

← The beam of Jim!

I just got off the philly flight to denver and the first dude i see is glomb. He Hands me the phone and insists i talk to brett micheals from poison to Get Vacu of jenna on the Poisoned Tour. Brett answe and asks how im doing. i said "Tell you th troth not very well im going to a rehab in Arizona. He said "which one"? I said "Sevra tu Hes told me he has been there and its not for me, i will be doing group activities li puzzles and water volleyball. and i'd be be off renting a harley, drive across country and clear my head. I took his advice only i rented a shitty chevrolet insted F-REHAB!

Shitbagged in budapest 05

I order stella artois wi

knowledge of bars—
a packed night club y
the dancefloor and
the heat of the mom
saver!

itty bit me! ↓

of Ice!

7 minutes after this taken photo I was outsid
Iron hill with a Zodiac Coke peeing on th
window suppose im not invited back?
I spilled my drink!

F $1.50

ed out if you
on chelantly pis
ows cause their
ing. Brilliant tim

long beach tradeshow - passed out in
front of hotel door and left Tim o'connor
and noof on the sidewalk. And left my
wallet at the reception! Tim called my
mom and said I was missing. she called
the cops!

soar
inal

ck
THE LATEST

Black/Slate          Black/Royal

at kind of shit are you trying to pull? You got cut
f just when that guy was going to fuck that slut
tch. The music started to play just as that guy put
 the rubber. I thought you could do and say anything
 satellite radio? WHAT THE FUCK!!!!????? I HOPE I
DN'T GET ROBBED BY THIS FUCKING SIRIUS SATELLITE
CKING RADIO!!

ILL A FAN....KEEP UP THE GOOD WORK.

Im sure at this point a lot of people must ha
and thought I was some spoiled brat ass kid
driving around some hot shit ferrari that my
would like to give these people a ~~reality check~~ News Flash
ACROSS THE STREET FROM A SHIT FA
sharing a bedroom with my brother and
regal that my aunt Boof gave me for 6
from a fuckin row house In Linwood, P
In jail! So if you happen to be one oc
something to say about the ferra

MENSIO

...ked at me
...rich family
...ought me, I
...ck – I LIVED
...FOR 20 years
...ly got a buick
...my relatives come
...half of them are
...ucks who had
...it my fuck!

Love,

BAM!

12    12A

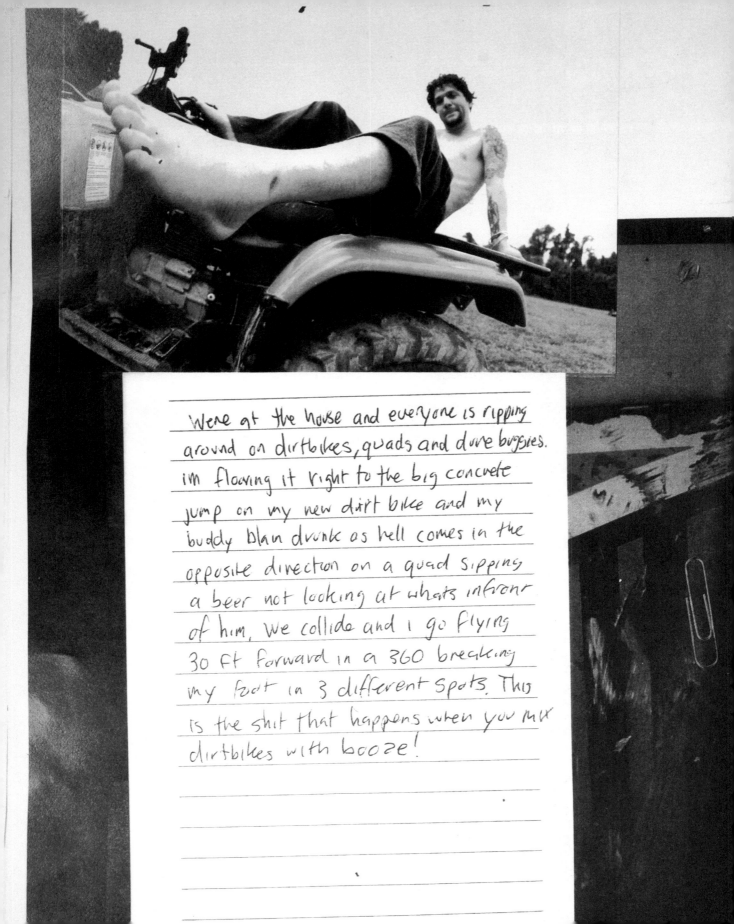

Were at the house and everyone is ripping
around on dirtbikes, quads and dune buggies.
im flooring it right to the big concrete
jump on my new dirt bike and my
buddy blau drunk as hell comes in the
opposite direction on a quad sipping
a beer not looking at whats infront
of him, We collide and i go flying
30 ft forward in a 360 breaking
my foot in 3 different spots. This
is the shit that happens when you mix
dirtbikes with booze!

This is the day I get slapped awake
by a strange film crew at 9am telling me
have to film CRIBS now. I tell them to
comeback tommorow, they say we came here
from NYC and you have to film this. So I
now get up, fix myself a beer and f
to get through this mess I got in! The
69 eyes show up as I am showing the ho
I get the bright idea to wake up now
with hot wax from a giant candle, I d
so, then force him to go on the rope sw
in the nude for cribs, once he agrees I
throw his sweatpants in the fire burr
only the penis area out of the sweatpan
now he is helping me show the new lamborg
off with his dick hanging out. Best cr
ever!

are, thats why you can buy it at Fuck(...)
nothing i get in return for playing you (...)

27. pharrell williams "if you gon't respe(...)
   be one!" VINCE NIEL K(...)
28. fuck dave mathews, fuck vince neil(...)
   of 3 stories breaking both of his (...)
   about at 50 Rockin and/or rollin(...)

28. Bucky lasek, Hawk, Penny, tom b(...)
29. PINK (cheapskates) LOVES HEAR(...)
30. Dont ask me about jessica sim(...)
   that name your camera is go(...)

31. Talent noticed Dico/Miller, told (...)
32. how did jackass happen?
33. drop in with Raccoon suit or a pai(...)
34. why is jackass so gay? no pants (...)
35. sieze the day (ville in lima) show (...)
36. Meeting jimmy for shopping carts (...)
37. VLB highlights (working with a crev(...)
   1. Europe
   2. delasno / danny way
   3. state of bam
   4. dont feed phil (Turbo)      why do you
   5. Brazil Helicopter             fuck(...)

arbucks, theres
POISON GIRL
illionaire you'll never
macay fell off
one more
made OK
Milk

The township is trying to tear down my new ramp because they say someone might fall on it. No fuckin shit! I fall on it every time I skate it! thats the whole point of skateboarding is to do as many tricks as you can till you fall Ma

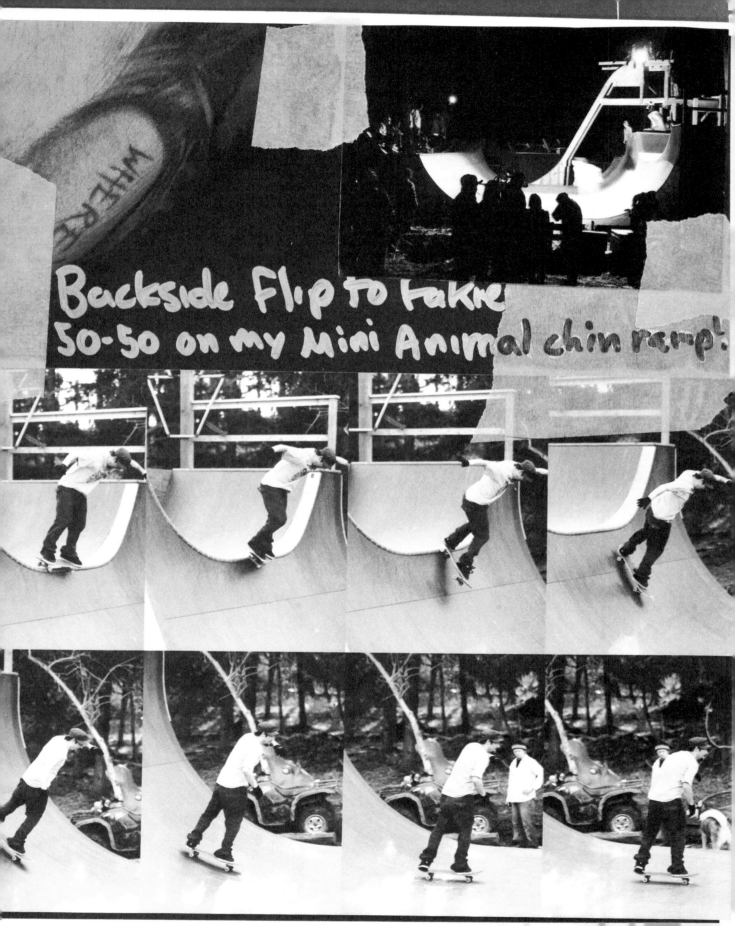

Backside Flip to fakie
50-50 on my Mini Animal chin ramp!

TROUBLE

KITTY KITTY KITTY KITTY!

CATALUNYA
SHITBUM

TROUBLE

MY CATS

MOUSEBREATH

MOUSEBREATH

←Tuna!

Meow Meow
kitty kitty
Meowmeow!

NOVAKS
Faggy!
Song.

Oh, me, and my buddy Bam!
walkin down the street
hand and hand until the
Bitter end, end, and,
Me, and my best friend
BAM!

Where he sits i'll
sniff where he shits
i'll sit. if theirs a
farty from his hiney
i will take a sniffy
wiff!

Novak once again brings a college girl home to hump and I tried to put a stop to it so I had Seth paint a gay mural in his bedroom - a Tom Selleck lookalike toying with a cock!
- Came home and had to explain himself to the girl, but wound up laid anyway →

NOVAKS MURAL ABOVE HIS BED! AHAHAHA! →

"oh yeah, so hard it fee
going to come out of m

Seth and i are sitting at the house bored to tears and novak went out to get some pussy at the bars. So Seth printed out a picture of tom selleck and painted a big mural of him sucking a dick above Novaks bed. Novak comes rolling in at 2am with a college chick. He turns on the lights and has to explain himself for 20 minutes B4 he got in her pants! AHAHA

ike its
-outh"

179

M Serveillence fight @ Rexs

HOTEL DE ROME

1. Managers / not pleased / get really
   BTS
2. Sing to songs in car
3. Barcelona/ Missy ne
   Cant take it a
4. kinghaz
5 ed

| | | | Price net | Deb ne |
|---|---|---|---|---|
| 03.01.06 | Communication Services VAT 22% | 1 | 1.66 | |
| 03.01.06 | Telephone Charges VAT 22% | 1 | 172.00 | 1.66 |
| 03.01.06 | Telephone Charges VAT 22% | 1 | 9.51 | 172.00 |
| 03.01.06 | Telephone Charges VAT 22% | 1 | 28.69 | 9.51 |
| 03.01.06 | Telep | | 10.66 | 28.69 |
| | | | 3.06 | 10.66 |
| | | | 3.06 | 3.06 |

that made a tent in his trousers, by putting some poo on a plate at a restaurant and complaining that

bastes and roasts himself. I get a terrible feeling. It's very scary. I have no earthly

wonderful at bathing parties...." Good, atmospheric stuff, and it gets

Telephone Charges VAT 22%          1

.06   Accommodation Package

.06   Communication Services VAT 22 1

.06   Telephone Charges VAT 22%     1

1.06  Telephone Charges VAT 22%

.01.06  Visa

Can take
shave them up her FU
Until she starts wor
girls easily forget
dollar! if that
she would comp
6.04.2009!

$1,700 →

GUMBALL RA

POWER'S LICENSE

www.state.pa.us

No: 25 153    Dups: 02
DOB: 09/28/1979   Sex: M
Class: C    Eyes: BL
Endorse:    Height: 5'06"
Com/Med Rstr: *I*
Issued: 12/03/2001
Expires: 09/30/2003

BRANDON C MARGERA
2 GRAYHAWK LN
THORNTON PA 19373

DL

$250,000 →

# Chateau Marmont
## hollywood

April 2006

Just got pulled over going 167 miles per fucking hour on the 10 freeway in Los Angeles with ryan Dunn. The cop gave me 5 citations - speeding

- wreckless endangerment
- no seatbelts

- passing people on the shoulder of an intersection

- beer in the car

I lost my liscence for 2 months but im still driving.

8221 SUNSET BOULEVARD   HOLLYWOOD CALIFORNIA 90046

TELEPHONE (323) 656-1010 FACSIMILE (323) 655-5311

| | | | |
|---|---|---|---|
| 2 3 4 5 6 7 8<br>9 10 11 12 13 14 15<br>16 17 18 19 20 21 22<br>23 24 25 26 27 28 29<br>30 31 | | | Restaurant festiva<br>IRON HILL<br>; KILDARES |
| **5** skated<br>Driveway<br>300 sit ups<br><br>CKY @ READING<br>Hopped on tourbus<br>w/MISSY<br>*Labor Day* | **6** chilled w/cky<br>IN NY<br>Bought Frassle rock<br><br>Sound check<br>CKY IN NY!<br>stayed at Carson<br>Dalys house | **7** 456 meeting<br>MTV meeting in<br>NY<br>Drove to west chester<br>watched Rosencern for<br>a dream<br>Jenn breaks into the<br>fucking house at 4am<br>COPS CAME | Private Jet<br>to<br>San Diego<br><br>ASR TRADES H |
| **12** drore home from<br>Ocean city NJ<br>Got Laptop @ apple store<br>300 sit ups<br><br><br>FIREWATERS, DUFFERS1<br>69 and Fucked | **13** Fly to<br>FT. WAYNE<br>INDIANA,<br>DINNER w/John Cougar<br>mellencamp | **14** 450 sit ups<br>Demo<br>FT. WAYNE<br>INDIANA | **1** 300 situps<br>fly to<br>CAYMAN<br>ISLAND<br>Skated the<br>BLACK PEARL |
| **19** Flew home from<br>ATLANTA<br>400 sit ups<br>Kerry came over<br>skated delaware w/Nate<br>RADIO BAM!<br>KOOMA w/Missy, Rog, Nate<br>BOWLING IN DOWNINGTOWN<br>HUGO POOL | **20** Season 5<br>Commentary for VL8<br>IN PHILADELPHIA<br>Meeting w/saturn<br>@ kildares<br>Went to Blarney st.<br>+ kildares | **21** peppermill w/missy<br>Got Message in wc<br>went to Birds+bees<br>fucked<br>Read novak book<br><br>went to Jess's | **2** Edit HIM docum<br>for MTV2<br>Got fitted for TUX<br>300 sit ups<br>Looked @ greystor<br>Mansion for CKY v<br>Goose cock<br>300 more sit ups<br>Kildares<br>Gregs house Ra |
| **26**<br><br>LA | **27**<br><br>did shopping cart | **28** | **29** Brandon Dicos<br>house<br>sushi |

pacific blue'
to brans
ted film documentary
meeting
orth w/ Antny bleedhw
's saw thieves

Gill
kerry airs

kings of prusse
Bought huge n
saw 40 yr ol
300 more si

**9**

Skated the
driveway w/R
Roof, Nite br
skated eas

an Diogo

Conecall (
Giveawa

Skate eas

watch Cino

o situps

16

500 situ

How many more ways

# BamMargera

ONTREAL
NEBEC

189

IM in Colorado filming a VLB episode Called "Groundhog day" and I cant drink for 10 days Cause im preparing To do the LOOP in Pheonix, AZ for the Tony Hawk boom boom huck Jam. We Are at copper MT. and Novak is passed out in the snow after dancing with his pants off standing on the bar. This will be my 3rd time trying the LOOP. I ate shit in florida for jackass, then tried it at bob burnquists and nearly did it but my legs were giving out on the 20th attempt so I had to stop. Now in 10 days im ginng it another GO!

ARIZO
Just la
the Loop
1st try af
tAking the p
away!!! 13th
Person to ever
it! wahoo! This
Mexican news report
wanted to Fuck me t
night but I got to
drunk and blew it.
Passed out in my ro
and woke up to a str
overweight girl on my
dick saying "I love yo
I love you! i love you!"
I flipped her off of me a
Screamed. She was the m
resnetful Hump ive eve
Fucked hands Down!

Listen to "Radio Bam" on Sirius Faction, channel 28. And sorry to crush any dreams, but he's been happily dating a high school friend for three months.

## DEAR MAN:
Bam Margera tells you b
use the boys for a night

**Q: Are there any trick phrases I can th
ing up a hot guy to ensure we'll be he
something besides, "I want to sleep
22, New York**

A: If you're at a bar, say, "I want to bu
Compliments on clothes, cool-looking
also good. You could tell him, "That's
does it mean?" That always works—I get stringed in
tattoos since I'm still totally stoked on all of them.
music for eight hours straight. But, yeah—don't say
Sometimes I run into sketchy rock chicks and they'
forward, like, "I wanna take you to my room." It wo
chosen different words. They make it way too easy—
You'd go up to their room, and you probably couldn
e worst—this girl walks up to me at a bar and sla
mped it on her head. Turns out she was a fa
ould enjoy it if a stranger smacked me i

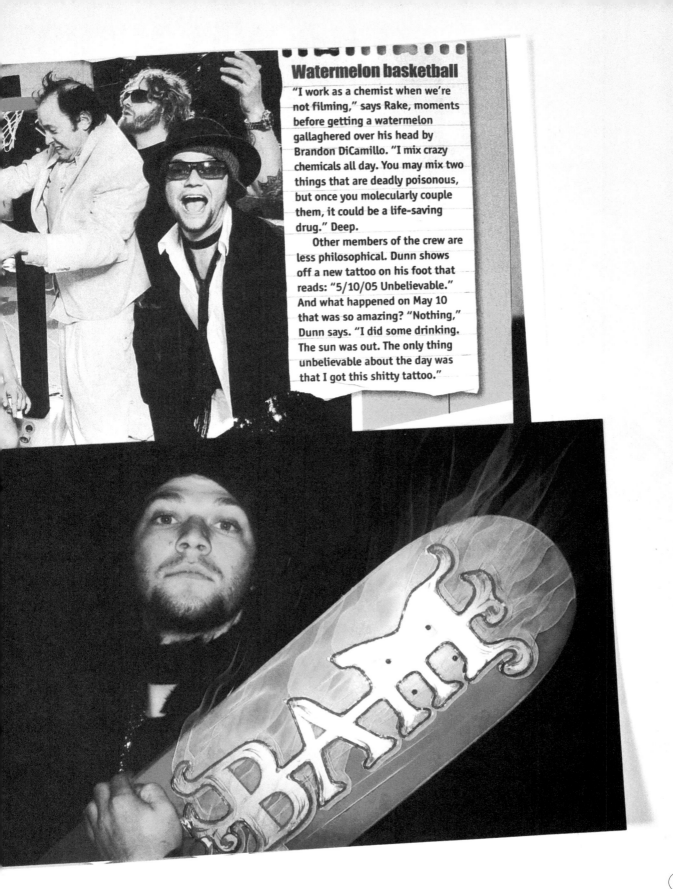

## Watermelon basketball

"I work as a chemist when we're not filming," says Rake, moments before getting a watermelon gallaghered over his head by Brandon DiCamillo. "I mix crazy chemicals all day. You may mix two things that are deadly poisonous, but once you molecularly couple them, it could be a life-saving drug." Deep.

Other members of the crew are less philosophical. Dunn shows off a new tattoo on his foot that reads: "5/10/05 Unbelievable." And what happened on May 10 that was so amazing? "Nothing," Dunn says. "I did some drinking. The sun was out. The only thing unbelievable about the day was that I got this shitty tattoo."

## F.D.R. WAS MY HOTT
## STARTED SHOWING

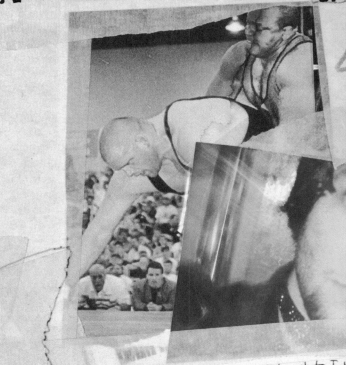

At the time of these Rake Yohn photo I w
the perfect heavy metal poster child. Thats w
on the cover of CKYaK! Now Rake is a chameo
him tuck his shirts into his khaki pants. Ahah

## NOW I HAVE MY OWN
## WHATEVER I WA
## I WA

OT UNTIL JERKOFFS
AND WOULDN'T LET ME
BREAK A SWEAT!!

BAM

ARK AND I CAN DO
AND INVITE WHOEVER
... AAAHHAHAHAHAHAHA!!!!!!!!

"yo dudes i got kicked out of school today!"

"your dad is gonna kill you"

CUT TO

"Get in the car ding bat"

"Back in the war we killed cissys like u"

---

"Cease and desist, u cant work on ur invention?"

CUT TO

"This means war!"

CUT TO

(CAR BARRELS THROUGH GARAGE)

CUT TO

"Dominick the filthy cronies are breaking into the werehouse"

Cut to

"That money is born to be mine!"
(knife hitting rut ru's face)

"sweet circonia Beast"
CUT TO
SHOOTING

---

Libby→ "Meet me upstairs in one of the bedrooms"

CUT TO

TUCKER AND BAGGER IN BED

Libby→ "What the hell is going on here?"

Ralph→ "I thought i found true love!"

CUT TO

Phil→ "hey bruno, its the gay gazette and hes on the cover!"

CUT TO

Don vito→ "My nephews gay!"

---

LENNY GOLF CART KICK →

★ CEASE AND DESIST, U CANT WORK ON Y INVENTION?
★ THIS MEANS WAR
★ PONCE ON FIRE
★ THIS IS MY KIND OF MOVIE
★ AMBULANCE HIT
★ DOM WICK WHAT ARE YOU MAKING US WATCH?

[THINGS TO THROW IN IF NEEDED]

A.) SCOTTY LEDUCHE SPINNING AND LAUGHING

B.) LENNY HITTING MACROGANS WALL

C.) TUCKER DESTROYING DINNER PLATES

D.) "THAT MONEY WAS BORN TO BE MINE"
(SHOW RUT RU WITH THE MONEY)

E.) "I HEAR YA'S TALKIN ABOUT ME IN THERE!"

F.) DUDESONS FALLING OUT OF TREE

6.) VITO DEVIL "RUT RU SUX"

H.) "TUCKER WERE CHEERING FOR YOU"

I.) Both needles in the ass.

---

Lenny → "YOU DO KNOW THERE IS A KN FIGHT AT THE TRAILER PARK"
(SHOW HAIN WITH THE SHOVEL)

Tucker → "I KNOW IM GONNA TALK LIBBY INTO LIKING ME AGAIN"

CUT TO

Tucker → "I MADE THIS FOR YOU"

Libby → "IT SUCKS"

CUT TO

BRUNO KARATE CHOP

hen a rich jerk seduces your mom and steals your cool invention,
it's time to get even!
BAM MARGERA PRESENTS
MINGHAGS
THE MOVIE!
m Margera Brandon DiCamillo Ryan Dunn Rake Yohn
rk The Bagger Don Vito Phillip Margera Sr. Brandon Novak
thie "Boof" Margera April Margera Phil Margera Gina Lynn
avid "Lord" Bottaro Angie Cuturic Ted Trullinger Missy Margera
ompton Ass" Terry Kennedy The Bloodhound Gang The Dudesons
riters / Executive Producers Bam Margera Joe Frantz Brandon DiCamillo
oduction Designer Seth Meisterman Director Of Photography Joe Frantz
RIGHT ©2007 FANNAVISION INCORPORATED. ALL RIGHTS RESERVED.

6.4.

We have 3 more days of minghags filming left and i have been shitbag wasted basic-ally the entire shoot and forgot missys birthday. She talked me into going to rehab in arizona, the same shit kate moss went to. now im on a airplane reconsidering this shit. I have a layover in denver and slomb is meeting me For the one hour i have to get the next flight to tuscon. i dont think rehab is for me, i will simply just not drink, i will find out my final descuion in 30 minutes when this flight lands. By the way i am writing this is cause the fuckass next to me wont stop talking And asking me dumb questuns. So much for First class!

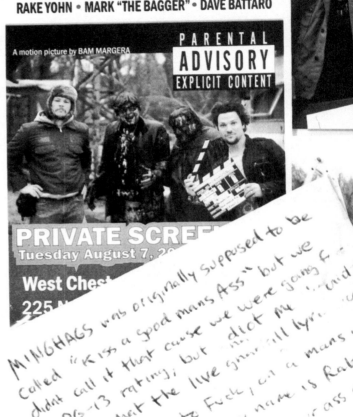

**MINGHAGS**

BAM MARGERA • BRANDON DICAMILLO • RYAN DUNN
RAKE YOHN • MARK "THE BAGGER" • DAVE BATTARO

A motion picture by BAM MARGERA

PARENTAL
**ADVISORY**
EXPLICIT CONTENT

**PRIVATE SCREE**
Tuesday August 7, 20

West Chest

225 N

MINGHAGS was originally supposed to be called "Kiss a good mans Ass" but we didnt call it that cause we were going f a PG-13 rating; but dict me and realize that the live group will lyr esre

"Im delicious to Fuck, eat a mans
I will suck, mark my name is Rake, f goodness sake, I will rape your ass every
And eat a cheesesteak"

That sentence right there will turn it
directly to rated R or NC-17 at the
what iN sam hell was I thinkin
up in finland

12)

13) fire

14) fati ice (controlled)
15) deliver a telegram with
hit Numbe teleopto to o
fus is a bird

ess, golf
down, edit,
golf to calm
Edit, stress
to calm down.

Tattersall reprezent!

D TO FIND 'BRUNO' FOR

think Frantz wanted to

OP frOm The BlooDhOUNd

OU'RE THE
BEST...
AND YOU
STILL ARE!

he totally aGreeS ....

STILL ArE - BRUNO

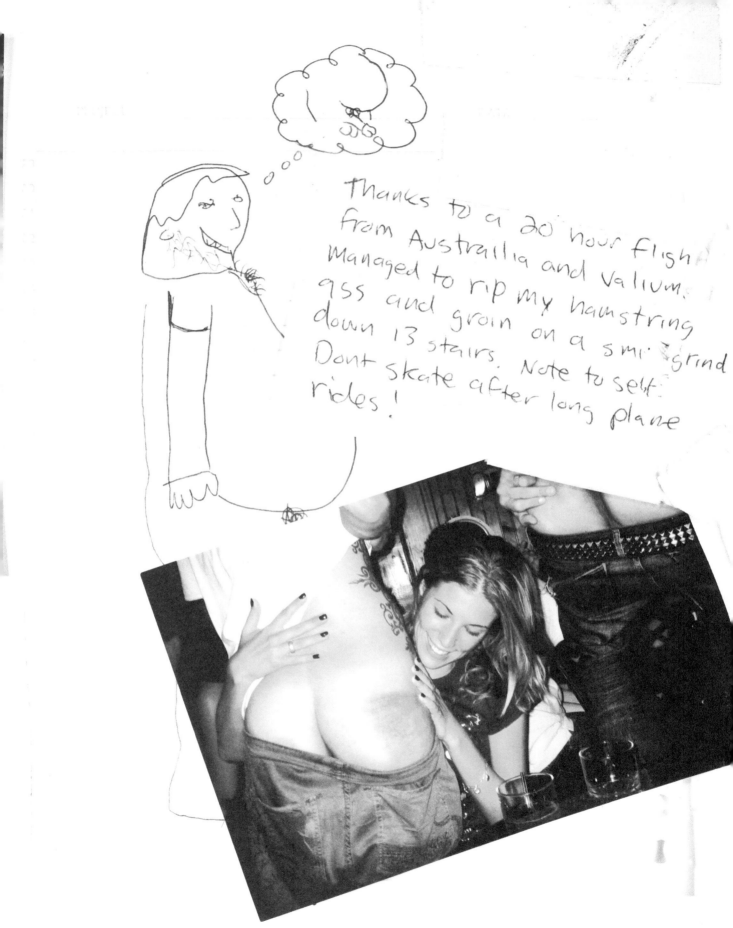

Thanks to a 20 hour flight from Austrailia and Valium. Managed to rip my hamstring ass and groin on a smith grind down 13 stairs. Note to self: Dont skate after long plane rides!

How can your stomach be Rumbling when you eat this much!?

① April 20-22  Louisville, KY  83

② May 18-20  Grand Prairie, TX   X-trials

③ June 15-17  Bristol, CT   X-trials

④ June 22-24  copenhagen, DE
    30-1  germany
  July 5-8  biarritz
    13-15  prauge

Aug 17-23  philly X-games

HAM BOX

3 loam boards.

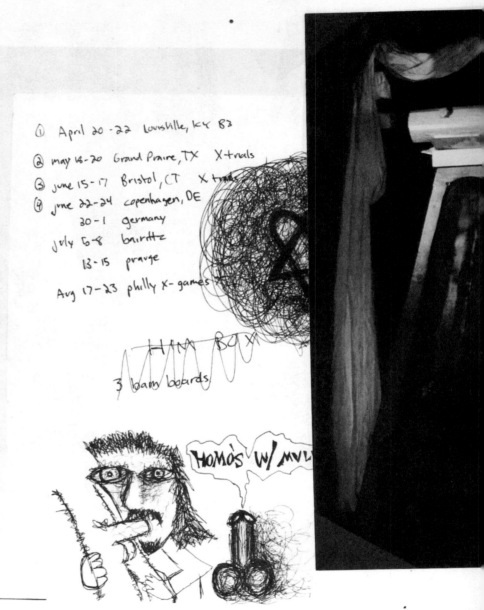

# MINGHABS

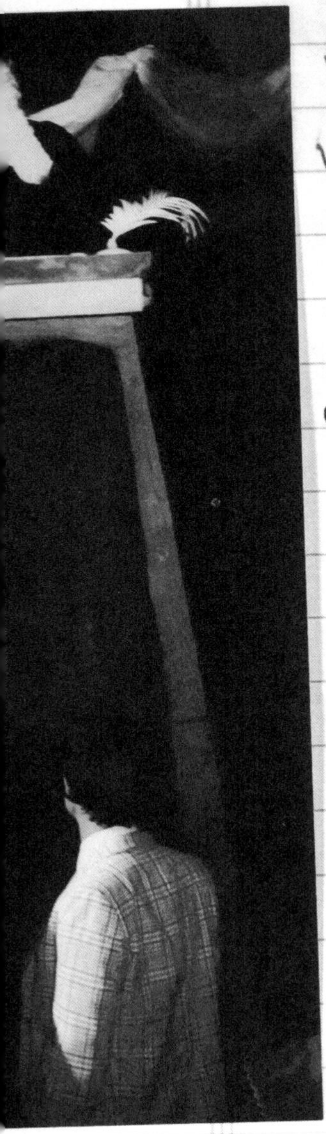

you are guilty

you owe the yuppie family one million dollars for disrupting their precious morning

you owe 8 million dollars for getting chocolate sauce all over the gays GUILTY

you owe 5 million dollars to Libby parents for the stupid thing turning into a vicious robot

court adjourned

Beware of
Killer

Yo Dudes I got
Kicked out of
Shool today!

would you eat her
out?
yep    no

Stoic

the
y!

MINGHENKS

[G]    [H]    [H]    [H]

7. **FILTERING**: After proper conditioning, the beer is sent through a filter [G] to remove all traces of the yeast before it is transferred to the serving tanks [H].

8. **SERVING**: Finally, the beer carbonation level is adjusted and it is ready to be sent to our taps for consumption. From start to finish our beers travel less than 65 feet. There's nothing fresher!

XS

ter PA 19380 610-696-7769

CEMBER

ved the show cheers you're gonna hate rexs

FRI
ITTER
RENAKED BUTHOLE
THE MILWAUKEES
TO FAR TO WALK

THE BOILS
Bad Idea
Broken Hero
THE NOID

USSA
Featuring Members Of
NISTRY TOMAHAWK JESUS LIZARD
JS CONTAGION
New Connection
HE DANGER O'S
Cheers Elephant

SAT
TOM MARTIN
JAWFAKER
(JAWBREAKER TRIBUTE)
THE MINUS SCALE

SAINT CAINE
FOSTERCHILD
stygian

15
BACKWOODS
PAYBACK
UNKLE MAT
AND THE
SHITBIRDZ
20
MOSES LIVINGSTO
AND THE
RAGGAMUFFINS
MCRA

OWS IN JANUARY

hange without us calling to let you kno

space.com/rexsba

MEANS
WAR!

SHELF.
DIENTS:
E USE no

1. Roosevelt swimmer bitch
2. Outside Magazine
3. Hawk/oldboy
4. V.O.J party
5. gumball lawsuit
6. pet pillow think it was
   Kat
7. Kildares muffin top
8. dilworth birthdays
   everyones fucking
9. into the wild
10. Billy idol xmas photo
11. drop dead virgin ls.

# IG MINGHAGS

Get in the car
Dingbat!

pissed all over

Sugar Maples at Huron Lookout, Gatineau Park ... ère Huron, parc de la Gatineau

**SAM • SAT**

**VEN • FRI** 6

Mont-Marts Waterfall

Le Quebec
TO
PHILADELPHIE

**JEU • THURS** 5

went shoppin and shit with missy in
**Quebec**

**MER • WED**

Rode the Fuckin 4wheeler
to the airport cause all
the cars were gone

Flew to
**Quebec CITY**
stayed @
Le Chateau
Frontenac

...erjall
...cription Ablal
...e by Carla
**57 CAFE**
...ny Syracuse TN 155y

element

tor has to sew on a ripped of dick
arn extra for a handling fee? Some
nk about!

**SHOOT** 2oo7

**Amy Harris**
Phone 3666 6016
Email harrisa@qnp.newsltd.com.au

**Phil Bartsch**
Phone 5584 2870
Email bartschp@qnp.newsltd.com.au

...TTED A STAR? GIVE US A CALL

Calvin

...street
...s, L-R, AJ
...ean, Howie
...ugh, Nick
...er and
...n Littrell

*Handwritten note:*

10·17·07

I took missy to Australia for 8 days thinking we would have some nice vacation time, instead it was me hosting 8 one hour countdown episodes for MTV, 7 phone interviews and 5 autograph signings down the east coast that were 3 blocks down the street. Each day was 4 to 5 hrs of signing. I barely even got to sk8. Luckly I bumped into Linkin Park the last day and I actually got to take missy to a concert and escape!

# Bam the man for local fans

SKATE king and MTV *Jackass* member **Bam Margera** made it to Brisbane yesterday for an in-store promotion although he acted, and was revered by the teenagers, more like a rock star than a balancing freak.

Bam, who had only stepped off the plane a couple of hours beforehand, walked into City Beach in the Queen St Mall with a drink, of the top-shelf variety, mind you, in his hand and a broad smile on his face.

The queue of teens lined up to see the cable TV personality snaked through the store and at least 100m through the mall.

Extra security had to be rounded up to handle the gathering and also to answer the store's shoplifting alarms which rang like a government complaints hotline.

By Bam's side was his wife of eight months **Missy**, whom he met when they were in seventh grade and was part of their reality MTV show.

"This is pretty amazing," said Missy as she panned the store.

"I've had about 30 or 40 jobs in my life from waitressing to being a nanny, but now I mainly assist Bam."

...e top
...posite
...rday
...Roar

...ton is
...nth

...my
...ng to
...to
...want
..."
...h her
...isit
...cs.
...it's
...'ve

...of

...30
...the
...wort...
...each...
...gemolo...
...valued. B...
...when, wit...
...remaining, ...
...still been unc...
...visions of a wa...
...down sink," said ...
...party planner. Alas, gue... number 307 claimed it in the nick of time.

In budapest, I met C.O.B.
inger Alexi @ Lobby bar and
we polish off an entire bottle
of tillamoe dew. I bet him I will
jump off the budapest bridge by
the end of the day for $200.
the next morning I see him and
he says "you owe me $200"
I say bullshit fagit i already
did it. Here's Living
proof!!

"His foot seems to be a magnet for pain recently," I said. "He just broke his foot in three places riding motorcycles."

"Oh, that sucks," Knoxville said. "He'll be so bummed because he can't skate."

"But the Hummer?" I said. I fucking hate vers, I had to know how to destroy them. "What do to it? Did you take a chainsaw to it?"

No, it was a Saw Gall? A Sawl? Saws All thing?" finally. "And you can saw through those sons hes pretty easy, you know? Just get a Saws All to a parking lot and have a ball."

Oh, that does sound fun.

But yet another thing I wish all those Bam fans would emulate is their hero's favorite pastime: skateboarding. It's way more fun than a "heartagram" tattoo. What the hell is a heartagram, anyway? I have to admit I kind of like the way it looks, but what does that mean, "sensitive evil?" That makes about as much sense as "compassionate conservatism."

"Do you even skate anymore?" I asked him.

"If I have twenty minutes filming break," he said, "I'll go skate the mini ramp with like Tim Glom, sometimes Tim O'Connor and Kerry Getz

are here. If I have a full day off I'll g and skate. That's the thing, I don't going into Philadelphia and skati and getting kicked out. Fuck, I'd the Philly park and skate all day kicked out. It's way more fun like unless I have like a month to ki go to like Australia or whatever city spots. I have all this footage t out right now. I'm really psyched o likes it so much they want to sav or something."

see me.

S18

Were on the South island of New
Zealand and I see this 50ft
bridge with a massive current lead
out to the sea. I didnt know how
deep it was, but I didnt care, wh
the fuck is the next time I will
be here? I asked my self. Fuck it
I jumped and slammered to the
bottom, 6ft deep! ow.

Pivotal moment, Brandon Novak, Oxford

I came up with a skit called the human raccoon, which basically consists of Punching your buddies eyes out till they are completely black and blue. Then put him in a raccoon outfit and paint his face. We did this with novak for jackass 2 but it never made it. All we got out of the deal was a cool radio show!

# AT STATE OF THE SPINE RAMP IN AVONDALE, PA

# SKATING THE STATE OF BAM

I'm on the tony hawk gigantic skatepark tour and we arrive to louisville kentucky at midnight, I know we have a demo infront of 5,000 kids the next day at a huge cement skatepark that I have never skated. So I want to cruise the park at night to get a feel for what were getting ourselves into tomorrow. Sure enough I head right for the 20ft tall full pipe and head forward it at full speed. Just at about 13 ft is where the over vert is and im headed right at it as my front foot slips of the board in mid air. I fly head first from 13 ft above knocking myself out unconcious. The whole team rushes down to carry me out of the gigantic bowl and rushing me to the hospital. I was cat scanned with a concussion and a ripped liver and they were not letting me leave until they knew it was healing. 3 days I was in that fucking hospital and I had to take a private jet home for $10,000 because I couldnt walk through the airport. definitely top 3 out of my worst slams!

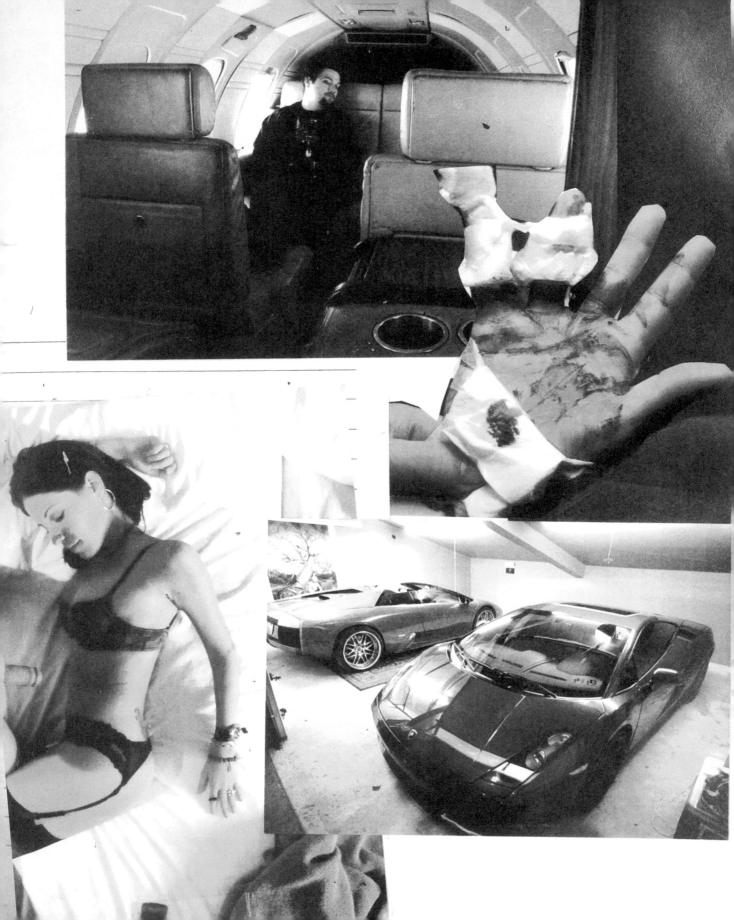

INJURIES!

I'm driving home from 50 cents house and eul juries
from the bloodhound gang calls and says there filming cribs
and for me to drive the banana car into the mote,
The mote was a 6ft drop and jared said its 7ft
deep. So I drive full speed into the mote thinking im
gonna get fucked up. Sure enough no injuries, so then
like an idiot I do a gainer off the top of the car and
underrotate causing me to go in head first. The fucking
Mote was only 2 feet deep! I cracked my head
open causing 15 staples in my fucking head!

Flew into Kentucky for an odio demo at a massive concrete park at midnight and I wanted to get a feel for the park before the big demo the next day. Its pitch black out and I go right towards the 20ft full pipe and go way over vert causing me to fall from 13ft above right to my fucking head knocking myself out and a ripped liver from the fucking ribs. Went to the hospital for 3 days and had a private jet take me home for $10,000 because I could walk through the airport!

The chronicles of
GNAR KILL!

DAVOS, SWIT

2003

B
A

ERLAND

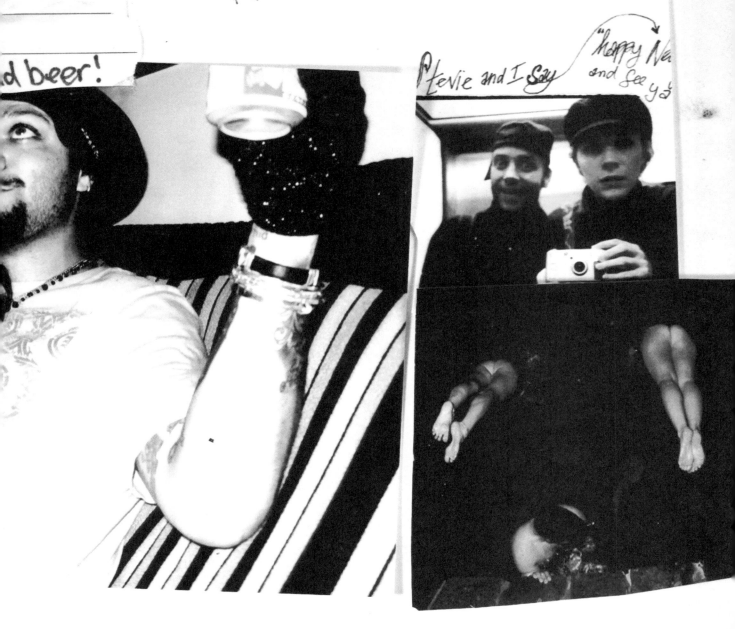

B+B,
good tidings I bring, to you and your si[...]
All the best in love + health —
Nice to know you
x Melissa x

Promises
drinkers
[...]sked, Red
had a
[...]rment
[...]er and
scared
[...]e. after
[...]r rehab.

d beer!

Stevie and I say    "happy Ne[...]
and see y[...]

BURNT FLOOR

1:15AM
FISH FRY TURNS INTO GLOMB FRY
ND DEGREE BURN ON THE NECK

So. glomb and
Camping trip t
Rushmore then h
Horse, Lake house g
caught 3 Fish, i
Prepares a fishfry
alone in a a millio
oil on the pan cat
Glomb drops the
curtains up in fla
Panicked and opene
throw the pan ou
wind blew mou
was a $10,000 mist
Parents. And the
It all is that I
DRUNK for on

OKABOJI

...ed to take a skate/
...ackhills to see int
...his girlfriends parents
... at lake okaboji. ne
... and 2 perch. Clomb
...e way we are completely
...take house) and the
...e, a big fire! And
...ting the couch and
...ng with his face. I
...ding glass door to
...a massive gust
...on more glass. It
...d pissed off some
...st thing about
...even Fve!

TED + KATAN Stuart,
thanx for letting us stay.
Sorry I almost burned it
down. Not a good first time alone.
Firemen here are nice though.
Steaks in fridge were a
pre-fire "thankyou". I'm sure
the floor + couch will require a
bigger "sorry" gift.
Tim + Bran

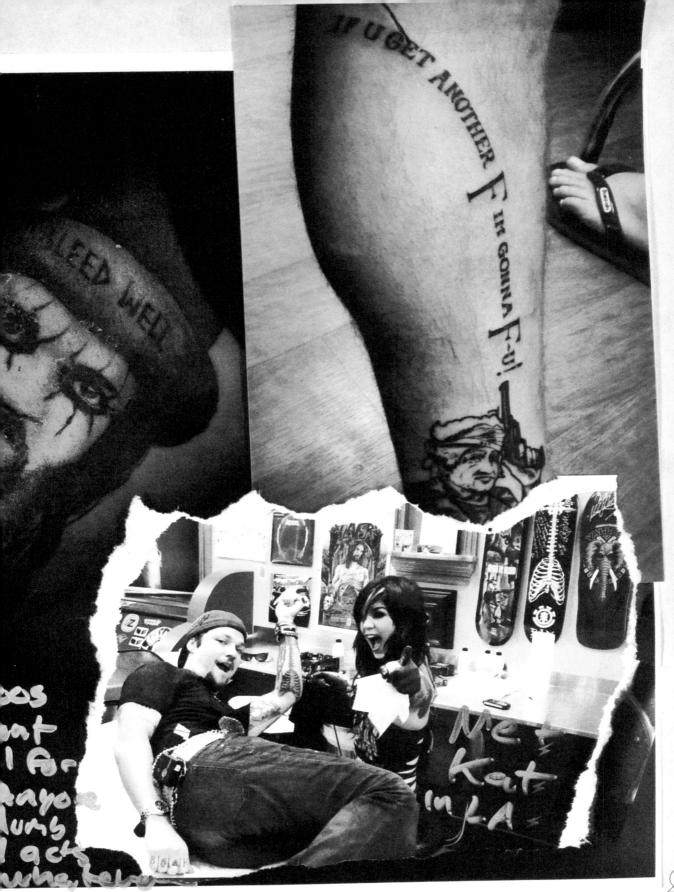

IF U GET ANOTHER F IN GONNA F-U!

BLEED WELL

Me + Kat in L.A.

I know what I want out of life, before I had too many things. Too many things that weren't mine and nothing mattered if something was broke, ~~and~~ it would just get replaced. I dont want a house decorated the way my mom wants it, I want to do it on my own. If you dont do normal things like Laundry, dishes, organizing your things then you will Pre occupy that time with something unproductive. Everything in This tiny Room in Barcelona is mine, I picked them out myself. The people in this house are hungry, motivated skaters who NEED to do the Next best trick to survive. I dont need fancy restaurants and I dont need to be at a bar everynight. I Need that time to think and skate the next day. I dont need medicine from the doctor to make me feel better. Skateboarding is my medicine? I need to use my legs as much as possible, Living in a city makes you do that and you will always experience something new and interesting even if you are walking the same route. I NEED TO START FROM SCRATCH AND REMEMBER WHAT ITS LIKE TO HAVE NOTHING!

# Day 2 (where the fuck is santa?)

We all have flights out of JFK at 8pm, I realize once again my fuckin passport is M.I.A., I rip my room apart digging through all my clothes for 2 fuckin hours and nothing. Now its 6am and I have to get into the production van to the passport agency in Philly for a $400 rush job. After 3 hours of bullshit I know have a new passport and get picked up in the hummer with The posse (CKY, Jess, Fanna, Novak, Frantz) off to JFK whe Fanna is shittossed from jameson and hes attempting to hit on girl, but his slurring words and knocking over some drinks got him nowhere! OFF to Finland!

LAYOVER AT LONDON HEATHROW 4 DAYS BEFOR CHRISTMAS DEC 21ST 2007

y 3 Hellzinki

arrive to Vaanta airport in
zinki at 10 am and the schedule
ight. The whole point of the trip
o make it 600 miles north to
arctic circle so theres no
me for sleep. Not to mention
re are a lot of rocker friends
mine to see. so First stop,
stvri, HIM's rehearsal studio
I can ask them For some
king advice to santas and
hear some like new rockin
shit'. Ville draws a map on
annas belly to show us the
ay but his sweaty belly was
sashing off the marker and
e werent about to be lost
n the middle of the arctic
woods in the freezing cold, So ville called his tattoo buddy
Juho to meet us at the top of tornii which is the tallest
building in Helsinki for Fanna to have a nice view
while we gave him the shittiest tattoo on earth.' way
to go!

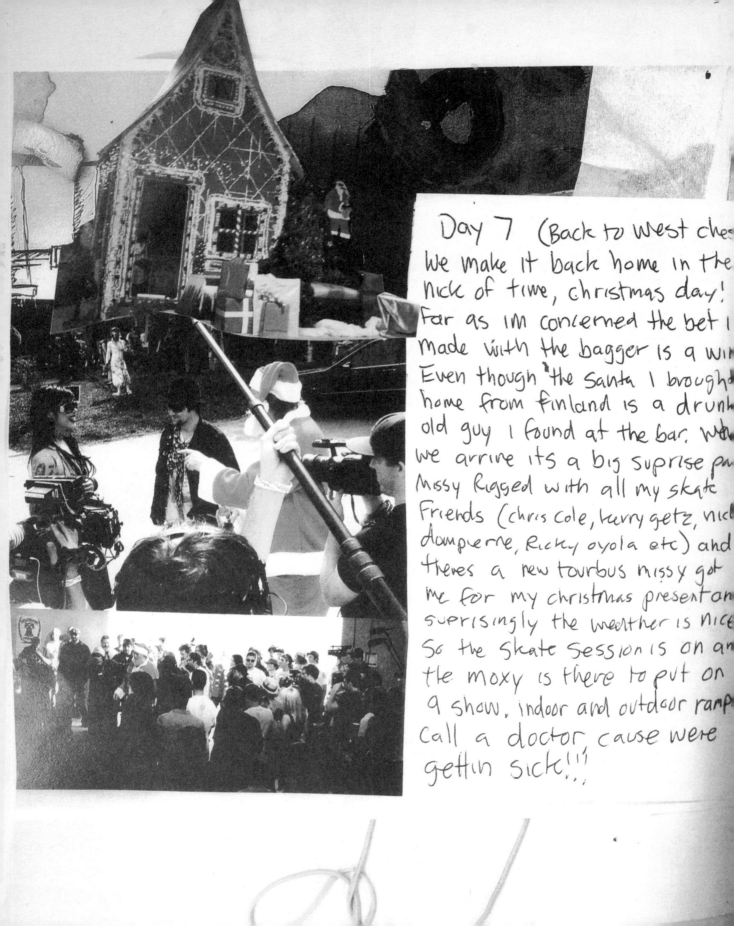

Day 7 (Back to West Che—
We make it back home in the
nick of time, christmas day!
Far as im concerned the bet i
made with the bagger is a win
Even though the Santa I brough
home from finland is a drunk
old guy i found at the bar. Whe
we arrive its a big suprise par
Missy Rigged with all my skate
Friends (chris cole, kerry getz, nicl
dampierre, Ricky oyola etc) and
theres a new tourbus missy got
me for my christmas present an
suprisingly the weather is nice
So the Skate session is on an
the moxy is there to put on
a show. indoor and outdoor ramp
call a doctor cause were
gettin sick!!!

It was Midnight and I was Leaving winkles house AKA the
Parallel skatehouse. I had 2 big bags filled with shit I bought
for Missy and a pair of all black half cabs. The First pair of
skateshoes I bought in 10 years and I was so stoked to skate in
them for the next week of filming with Kerry Getz in Barcelona. I
was the first time I had to walk alone at night, it was a
2 mile walk through some alleys and then up a windy Hill to
Fancy hotel miramar. As soon as im out the door i make eye
contact with some shady fuck walking in the opposite direc
think to myself why do I think this guy is going to follow
shade enough i turn around to tal

a quick peek and what do you know, he's now following me and there's not a person in sight. The worst part is I know I have to make a left onto a darker alley for blocks into a shadier part of town. I start walking faster and so does the cocksucker who wants my bags. Now I start running and he does as well. I finally make it to the massive steep hill that is about a mile up and my legs are giving up from all the skating we've been doing all day. I stop to think as this dude is coming closer and closer. Fuck it! I just started running, I sprinted up this steep ass hill until he finally gave up. I made it to the bad Hotel with jello legs but I still have my New skate shoes!

Note to self - dont walk alone at Night with a city your not familiar with. Especially when your carrying shit you really like !!!

Jackass week Radio faction

Finish it
In Spain
and s
. to
ch
A so

__ superstar - wake up dead
__ - the tweaker
__ - Life burns
__ you lived
__ down

a damn

P.S. If your in Barcelona, go to the Bottom of monjuic mountain and try sprinting up that shit with 2 heavy bags. It's a pain in the ass, it sucks and You'll hate it!!

So the hessians just finish the death gap on the mini ramp the day before my wedding. Tony Hawk arrives which is a good reason to start a session & try this sketchy shit. After 2 attempts Birdman finally pulls it off which means Im next. First try I eat some pretty good shit but on the third attempt its a make. Now its novaks turn. I can clearly see he is terrified to do it but after taking advice from Tony Hawk for 10 minutes you have to give it a try or your a full blown pussy and wasted his time. So novak goes for it and jumps off in the middle breaking both of his ankles. Now hes in a wheelchair in my wedding, And his only response is "free pain pills the hospital!"

Department of Elementology

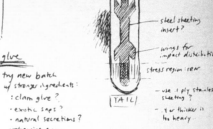

NOSE!
stress resin front
steel sheeting insert?
wings for impact distribution?
stress resin rear
use 1 ply stainless sheeting?
4 or thicker is to heavy
TAIL!

glue
try new batch w/ stronger ingredients:
: clam glue ?
· exotic saps ?
· natural secretions ?
· chewing gum

13 coil galvanized coiled springs

insert before.

FUUUCCCKKK!!!

try harder

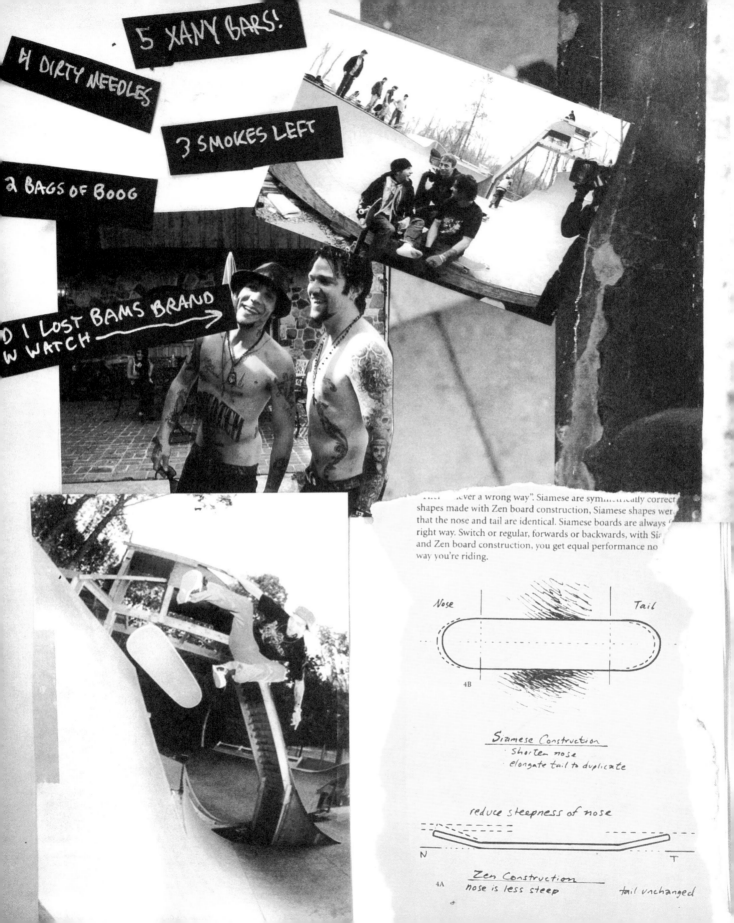

5 XANY BARS!

4 DIRTY NEEDLES

3 SMOKES LEFT

2 BAGS OF BOOG

1 I LOST BAMS BRAND W WATCH →

...ever a wrong way". Siamese are symmetrically correct
shapes made with Zen board construction, Siamese shapes wer...
that the nose and tail are identical. Siamese boards are always...
right way. Switch or regular, forwards or backwards, with Sia...
and Zen board construction, you get equal performance no...
way you're riding.

Nose          Tail

4B

Siamese Construction
· Shorten nose
· elongate tail to duplicate

reduce steepness of nose

N          T

Zen Construction
nose is less steep          tail unchanged
4A

Lou
Goyle!

My Name's Louie
I'm in the Moxy
And one day
I will play at
the Roxy.
My Names Louie,
I wear chinese
sneakers!

...m in New hope at chads
...ng to New cky songs live!
...e next day (we stayed over)
...has a 104 fever and...
...s Practice, now, we have
...ther option than to drink
...r and iced teas at
...and peters. Lawrence,
...Lou goyle decides to
...every drink that I get.
...keep in mind hes 23,
...29, So i know the drill.
...nds up barfing in the
...s and then passes out!
...railroad tracks in the
...s, Like ray brower,
...of sort of, this is
...n on sentence, anyway
...he is, as ray brower

**AND BY ME!** ➔

Its 11am on a hot summer day and I come down from my room looking a 6 dudes crashed on the couches and floor. Muse have been from the rager last night, well why not continue the mission. As i crack open a Pbr tallboy and people start to wake up I get the bright idea to go to the junk yard to buy 8 cars for $8,000 as glomb builds me a launch ramp over the garage, yes thats right! we are going to Put bricks on the gas pedals of cars and launch them over the garage! hours later we comeback with a shitload of cars and were ready to rock. I forgot to mention i had just broke up with my now X-girlfriend and all of her stuff is in bags in the gara who would have thought that the very first car we try misses the entire ramp and plows through the garage Sideways knocking every last paint can into the X' shit. She shows up the next day looking at the damage calling me everyo name in the book. i tried to tell her we were simply trying to Launch cars over the garage and she simply wasnt buying it. But fuckin hell it was the actual truth. By the way the 5th car jump was golden!!!

I decided to fishtail the limo into the pool and it worked beautifully. But I was not satisfied, so I started up shitbirds jeep and drove that in as well. Bad move. I owed him $2000! that piece of shit aint worth that!

CAMDEN TOWN 3:45 am – this dipshit moron idiot comes to london with $50 dollars in his pocket and spends it all on 8 boxes of Kentucky fried chicken for 3 people. What a shithead! The other 5 boxes we left there. I hope a few bums ate it! fuckin idiot!

NOVAK'S NEW VITAMIN: CABERNET SAUVIGNON
TIERRA ANTICA CHILE 2007

kensingtonroom
131-137 Cromwell Road
London SW7 4DU
T +44 (0)20 7598 7979
D +44 (0)20 7598 7980
F +44 (0)20 7598 7981

book@kensingtonrooms.co.uk
www.kensingtonrooms.co.uk / .com / .net

HOTEL – BAR – VENUE

CAMDEN TOWN
SHOPPING (LIKE ZOMBIES)
HOLIDAY INN (SLEPT 'TIL 7:30
ti Sushi (TIGER BEER
+ CABERNET

Now im sitting on a train[in?]
Wolverhampton waiting for
[th]e bar to open. its 11:30am
[an]d im starting early with red
[wi]ne, And i will tell you why.
[i] have been up since 4am calling
[Jy]rki, Jussi, Timo, Tina, Missy
[an]d know one knows how to
[an]swer the fucking phone. I have
[no] clue what hotel the 69 eyes
[ar]e at and theyre tourbus
[le]aves at 11:30. Finally at 11:30
[i] get a call back from jyrki
[tel]ling me the guitar techs flight
[ha]s been delayed from finland
[an]d they cant make it to camden
[tow]n in time before the download
[sh]ow. Now im on a trian smelling
[th]e whif of novaks 3 old day socks
[an]d im gonna throw up the 45 dollers
[of] KFC novak bought when he was
[dru]nk and searching for coke in SoHo!

THE 69 EYES

**London** Underground ⊖ London Underground ⊖ London U[nderground]

16 JUN 09          01DAY  TRAVELCARD   STD

16 JUN 09                    »12«

⋇          .==DAY TRAVELCARD OFF-PEAK

178839  02  0562   16JUN09 1241   £5:60C

[N]ot for resale        This side up · Not for resale        This side up · N
[c]onditions - see over   issued subject to conditions - see over   issued subject to c

Camden hotel logic! NONE!
So we barge into the hotel and
the doorman insist that we are
not staying there, I say "yes we
are here is my room key and its
room 405." The asshole still doesn't
believe me and threatens to call
the police if we dont leave, Plus
Novak keep chiming in threatning
to call his lawyer and makes
matters worse, I try to head for
the elevator and the dude is
not having it, now we are fighting
over my room key, Fighting!!!
Then another guy from the backroom
doing research on us tells the
guy that its legit and we are
staying there. He gives me my key
Back and I say "fuck you asshole
HA!" then i slam My door and call
Him an asshole once more, HA!

# CAMDEN TOWN · LONDON '09

"I WANNA BE BAD, I JUST DON'T WANNA GO TO JAIL — NOWACK"

"I MIGHT JUST GO TO DIE HERE"
— NOWACK

"THERE IS ONLY 7 PEOPLE I'LL
MISS, 1. MOM
      2. LIFE PARTNER
3½ BUCKY _ 3 DIVA
      4 & 5. BROTHER & SISTER
      6. MANDY
      7. BILL BUTLER
                    — NOVAK

"THERE'S NOT EVEN
A NUMBER ON THE MAP OR IN THE
EXISTING GALAXY FOR DELAWARE
WHORE TO HAVE A SPOT"
                    — NOVAK

"SHE WASN'T AS GOOD AS
THAT TEXAS BITCH
                    314 - 368 - 1977"

# The 69 Eyes music video

## Dead Girls Are Easy — W.C, PA

concept was fun and simple, 4 hot vampire chicks fucking with a nerdy convenient store worker, and they steal him and give him a night out on the town. Sexiest video ever!

**BACK IN BLOOD**

BABY VAMPIRE!

← Caddyshack
Convenient
Store
on RT. 1

After 69 eyes video PA!

I trusted #1 MIL

OIDE Here, This is the kind of shit that makes you quit drinkin,

:7am Right before Jaces BAR!

I didnt mean it, I swear, i mean, Maybe, well, it was on purpose!

DE ✓ Bum...

7 am all night bender with Mankawk, V, olde Jicuso, Frantz (who was a piece of shit) anyway. It was 7 am and we make it to my house and the fine idea comes up to put a glolf ball between oldes ass, Now, I can do it right, or I can do it wrong and make great! - So what do I do? I ack him in the ass as hard as I can and this is what happens ladies and gentelmen!

FUCK ME!

RED MOHAWK GEOFF'S PHOTOS

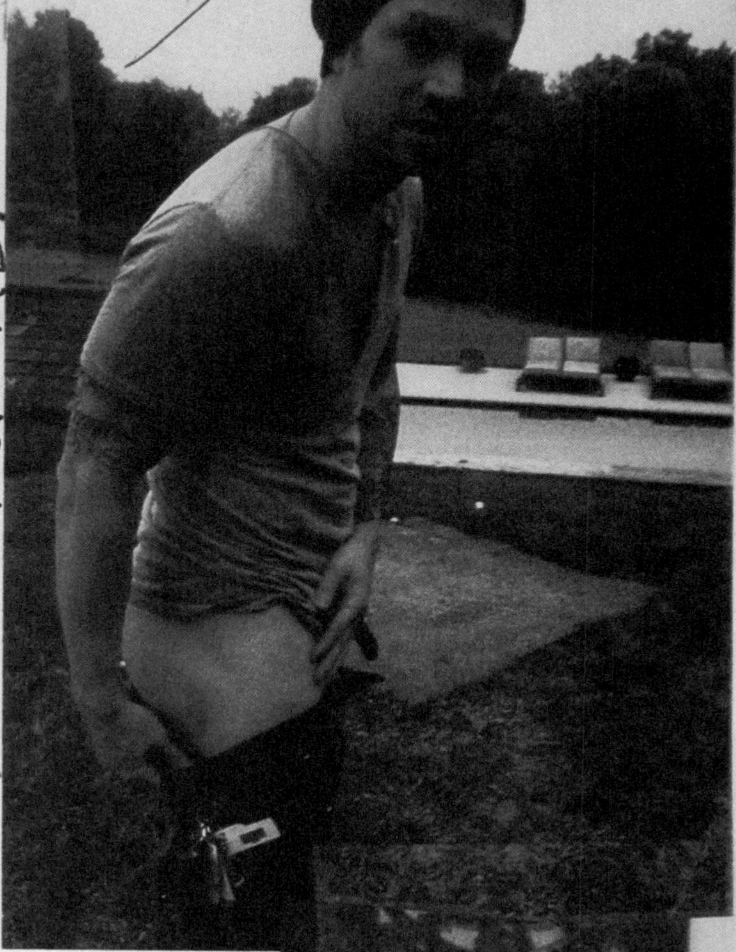

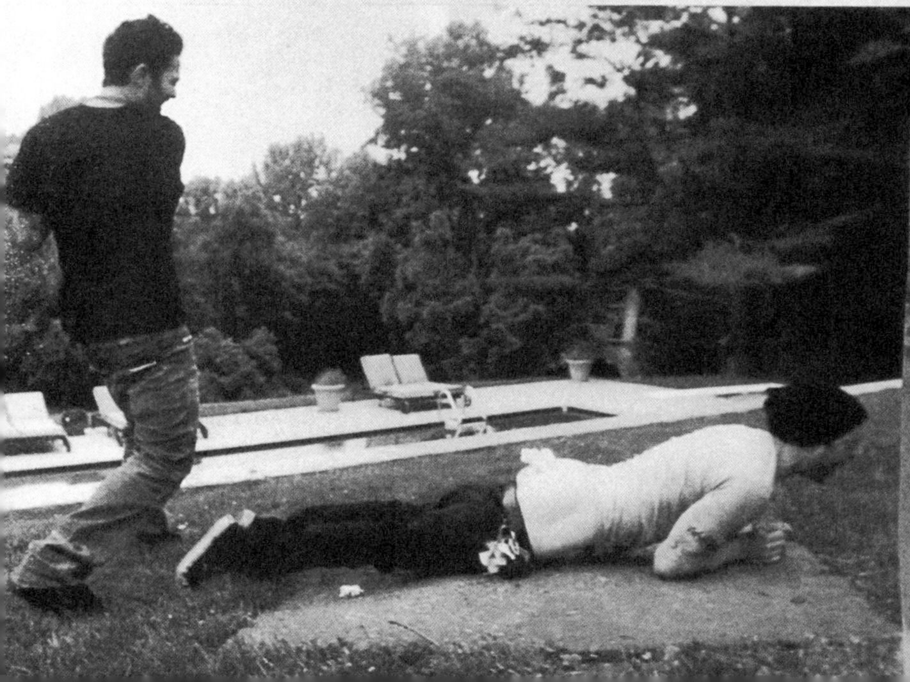

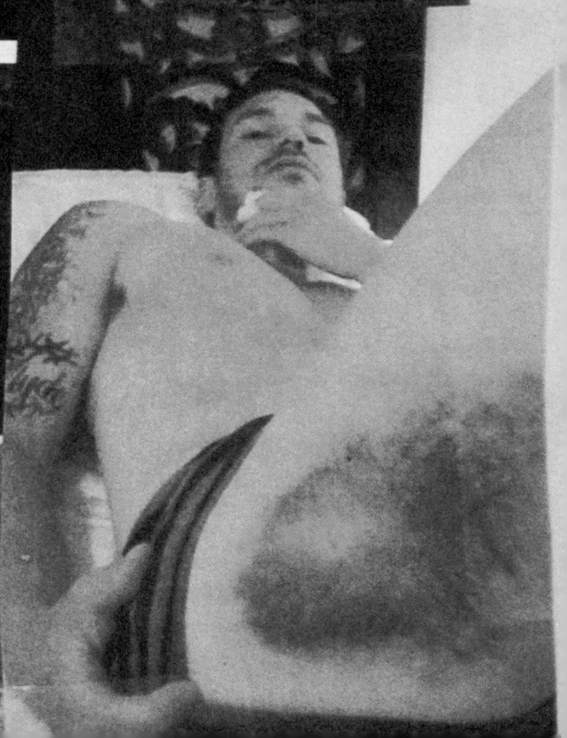

NOWAK·ME·VILLE

across the street from charlotte st. hotel ... I am banned passing in the basement 7 fucking years ago. they st... cant get in it. so we're across the street!

Metal Hammer awards—
I am getting ready to present
an award for anvil and
Nowak is blacked out drunk
with his ass hanging out
insisting that a 40 year old
gives up her panties so his
dick and ass wont hang
out anymore. Now I have
to leave with jussi to do
photos and press so I
dont know his condition
when I get back. Now
hes on a search for
coke at the steel panther
after party and I insist

That he does not do
it because its 3 am and
the night is officially
over! plus we are meet-
ing Ville at noon amoro
n Soho. So what does
he do? a fat rail at
3:30 am and i tell him to
fuck off and roam the
streets of london and
me! He shows up at 5am
banging on the door and
falls asleep instantly snoring
which drives me nuts.
Because i was almost asleep
now i have to listen to this?

So now i turn on the
tv to drown out the
sound, then i hear a new
noise, its him jacking
off! uhhhh, what a
scumbag, i should have
just knocked his lights out
and put it to an end!

TO THE
GOLDEN GODS 2009

FEATURING LIVE
PERFORMANCES FROM
TRIVIUM

ANVIL

COMPERE
JASON
ROUSE

AMON AMARTH
DevilDriver
SAXON
金 神

METAL HAMMER
GOLDEN GODS
2009

MONDAY JUNE 15
DOORS 6PM, LAST ENTRY 6.45PM

indigO₂ at The O₂

NORTH GREENWICH,
LONDON

VIP TRANSPORT
BOAT LEAVES FROM TEMPLE PIER AT 4.30 SHARP

Zille Zalo
00 358400 15███

Business Cards are FREE at www.vistaprint.co.uk!

# Red WiNE diaries of Novak

Freddie Mercury and Novak on the tube to Tottenham court rd! He frenched his 3 sided dick duster as he was reading gay shit!

So Novak shows up to Crowbar asking where the fuck pete doherty is, doing that is asking at Landmark where Ben Mason is, they dont like it. Its jealous fratboys. But in this case its wasted up rockers who are jealous he is successful and they aren't. We did a carbomb with the owner and staff and made him shut the fuck up!

## The Crobar

Its like a dark hole of fantastic grit and piss. Walls to wall pages of comics cover God knows what bodily fluids, Music at a volume! ah fuck yea and dark enough to realize your about to piss yourself and aint nobody gonna care

CROWBAR · SOHO · LONDON 6·12·09
So I'm back at the crowbar,
I don't know where the fuck 69
eyes are, and my phone doesn't
fucking work here. So I'm 99%
fucked. I order 3 red wines and
the bar tender reminds me how
I had to hide upstairs for 3
hours waiting for the cops to
dodge me because I jumped off
the top of astoria at a HIM show
3 years back and lost my shoe
kelly osbourne bet me I wouldn't
do it but I did. and the shoe
I lost is hung up at this
very bar. Not to mention.
My passport is a missing.
So lets rock!

VILLE
VALO @
fitzroy
pub

Wolverhampton TAXI piece of shit who jipped
US!!

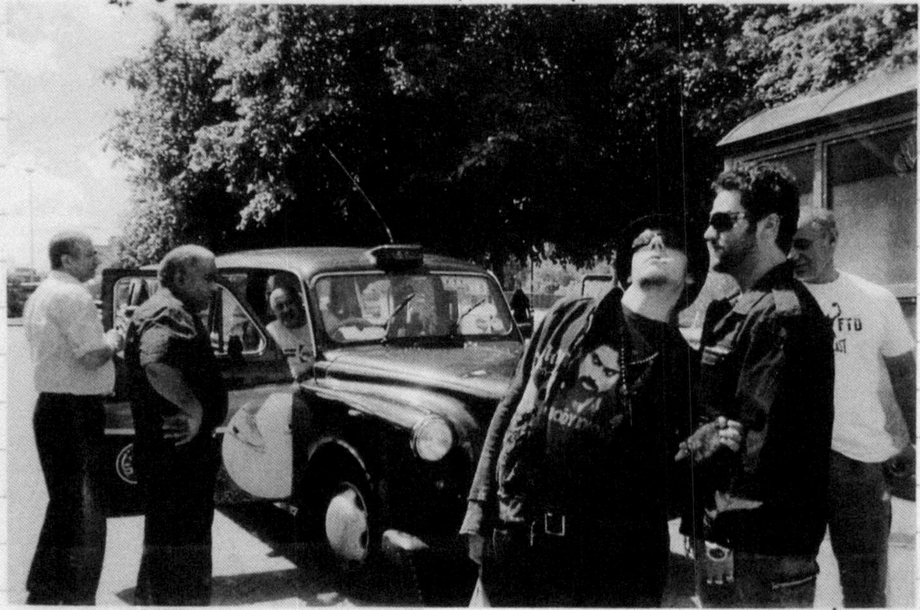

This fucko
took us 2 hours
the wrong way
plus got stuck
in an airshow
traffic jam and
we had to
get out and piss.
I smoked in his
cab and said
Fuck You.
He deser
It!!

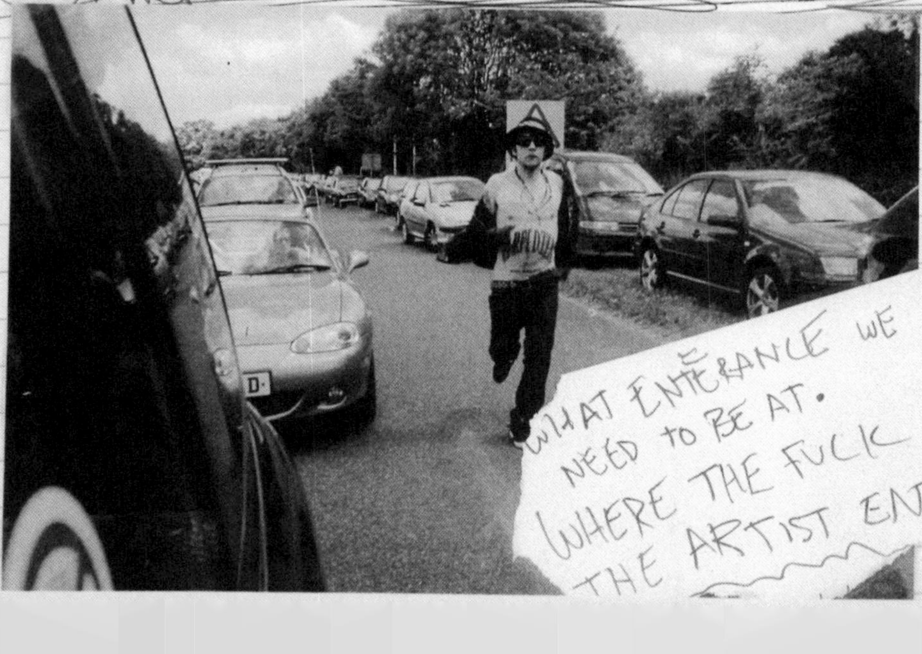

WHAT ENTERANCE WE
NEED TO BE AT.
WHERE THE FUCK IS
THE ARTIST ENTERANCE

# DONNINGTON · ENGLAND '09

Download festival —
So we are now forced to
take a train from camden
to wolverhampton, then
a cab to donnington, well
apparently theirs 2 fucking
donningtons because the
duckface cab driver took
us 2 hours in the wrong
direction through major
traffic because of an
Airshow. Once we get there
Absolutely no festival is
happening. I flip out and
light a smoke in his cab, he
tells me theres no smoking.
I tell him to fuck off

STEEL PANTHER

"ASIAN HOOKER!"

DONNING LOAD FEST

nd take me to the nearest train station, the next
rain doesnt leave for 2 fucking hours and it's
ot even in the right direction. Now I get another
ab 3 hours back to the real Donnington and spend
700 pounds getting there. We get there in the nick
of time for clutch, 69 eyes, Steel panther and
Def Leppard. Novak got jacked off by a floozy
and missed Def leppard. Then a long drive back to
London with 69 eyes with no beer. Another 300
guid. England is expensive! By the way I introduced
Steel panther to the stage And kicked novak in the
face, half the people thought I kicked tommy lee because
of novaks belly tattoo. They told me it was fucked up,
BUT its NOVAK!!

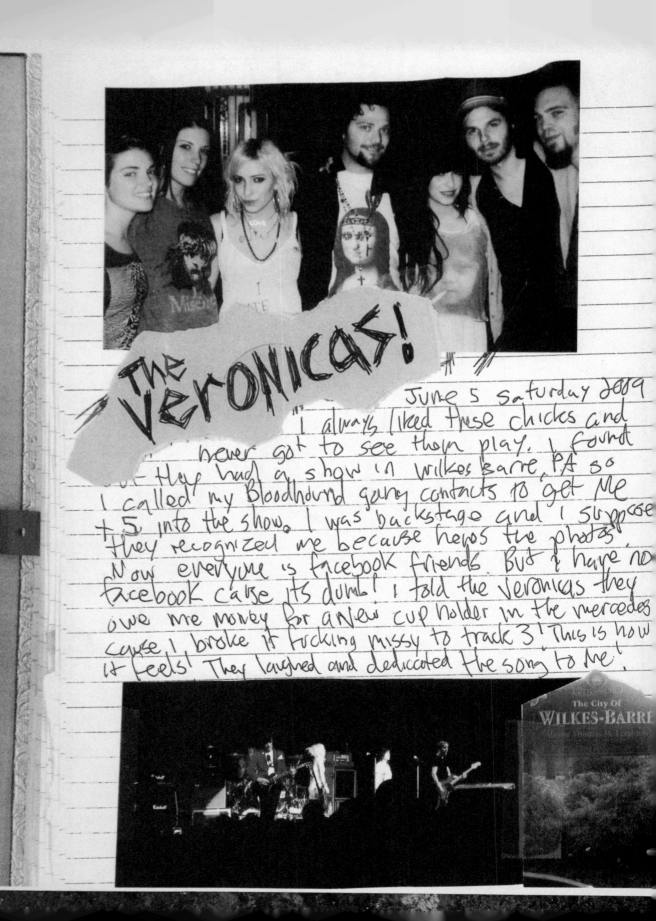

# THE VERONICAS!

June 5 saturday 2009

I always liked these chicks and never got to see them play. I found out they had a show in Wilkes Barre, PA so I called my Bloodhound gang contacts to get me + 5 into the show. I was backstage and I suppose they recognized me because heres the photos! Now everyone is facebook friends. But I have no facebook cause its dumb! I told the Veronicas they owe me money for a new cup holder in the mercedes cause I broke it rocking missy to track 3! This is how it feels! They laughed and dedicated the song to me!

The City Of WILKES-BARRE

# The Agonist

June 6 Sunday 2009!

So I meet this band at the note and think its one more night of ordinary bands, but its not! its basicailly in my eyes cradle of filth with a girl singer with blue hair named Alyssa. I say - Rad show, where are you off to and where are you staying? she says 'viterally in a Walmart parking lot in a van. I say, well thats not happening cause your all coming to my house! they come back and we hop on the quads at 3 am, the dune buggy had a head on collision with a tree, $4000 in daunages, another day at the house. Well this is them rocking in Allentown, PA. they are from montreal, home of borguts!! By the way they can stay at my house whenever they like! I love them!

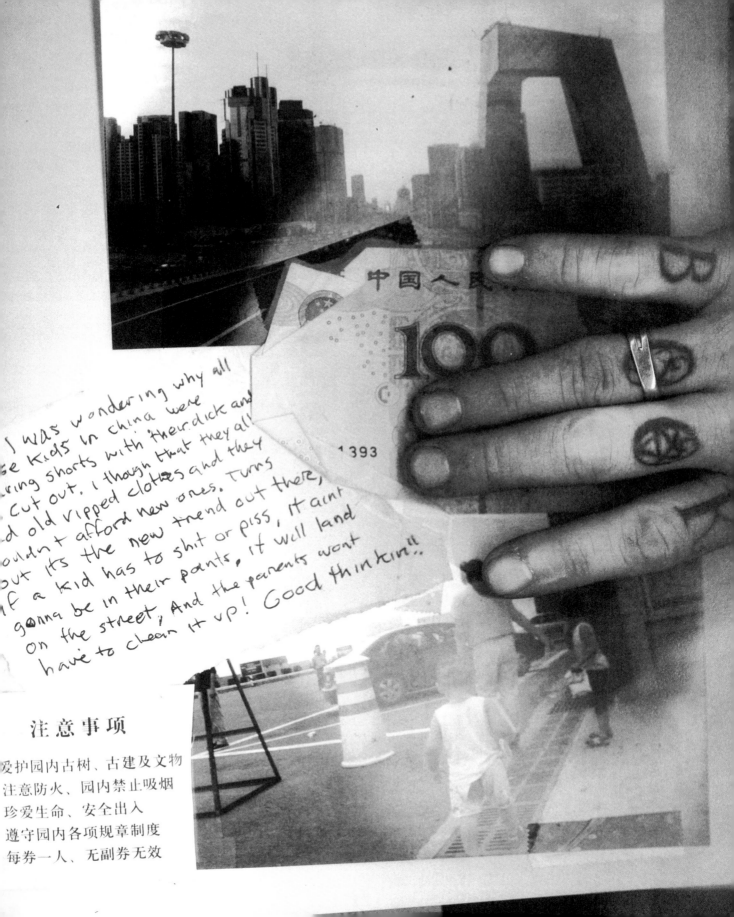

PHOTOS BY: RYAN GEE, ADAM WALLACAVAGE,
JOE DEVITO, ROGER BAGLEY, MARK WEISS
REDMOWHAWK GEOFF, CLAY PATRICK, JEFF TAYLOR,
BAM AND MISSY MARGERA